More Praise for *Gender Failure*:

"This book profoundly changed my life; I will step into the word and lexicon of 'gender' differently, I will never be in my body in the same way, I am a different reader forever, and I am grateful. Gender Failure *will take you apart and put you back together—I laughed my ass off, I cried my heart out, I yelled my head off, and I ended up in the only place that matters: love, compassion, with our whole bodies.*" *—Lidia Yuknavitch, author of* The Chronology of Water *and* Dora: A Head Case

"Gender Failure *accomplishes the impressive feat of adapting a live multimedia performance into a book. Rae and Ivan create intimacy through their charming, insightful, and sometimes painful storytelling, and I even found myself wanting to sing the haunting handwritten lyrics. Most compelling are the surprising moments of hope that help illustrate how defying gender is not a failure at all—but rather something to celebrate.*" *—Vivek Shraya, author of* God Loves Hair

Gender Failure

RAE SPOON

IVAN
E. COYOTE

Arsenal Pulp Press   Vancouver

GENDER FAILURE
Copyright © 2014 by Ivan E. Coyote and Rae Spoon

ARSENAL PULP PRESS
Suite 202–211 East Georgia St.
Vancouver, BC V6A 1Z6
Canada
arsenalpulp.com

The publisher gratefully acknowledges the support of the Canada Council for the Arts and the British Columbia Arts Council for its publishing program, and the Government of Canada (through the Canada Book Fund) and the Government of British Columbia (through the Book Publishing Tax Credit Program) for its publishing activities.

Earlier versions of some stories by Rae Spoon appeared in *First Spring Grass Fire* (Arsenal Pulp Press, 2012).

Lyrics and chords from "Ghost of Boy," "Joan," "Cowboy," "Gender Failure Theme Song," "Who Do You Think You're Fooling?" and "dangerdangerdanger" copyright © Rae Spoon 2014.

Book design by Gerilee McBride
Cover illustration by Claude Förster
Interior illustrations by Clyde Petersen
Photographs by Adam P.W. Smith
Editing by Brian Lam

Printed and bound in Canada

Library and Archives Canada Cataloguing in Publication:

Coyote, Ivan E. (Ivan Elizabeth), 1969–, author
     Gender failure / Ivan E. Coyote, Rae Spoon.

Issued in print and electronic formats.
ISBN 978-1-55152-536-5 (pbk.).—ISBN 978-1-55152-537-2 (epub)

     1. Coyote, Ivan E. (Ivan Elizabeth), 1969–. 2. Spoon, Rae.
3. Transgender people—Identity. 4. Transgender people—Canada—
Biography. I. Spoon, Rae, author II. Title.

HQ77.7.C69 2014   306.76'8092271   C2014-900270-X
                                                 C2014-900271-8

Contents

Acknowledgments

I would like to thank Brian Lam and all the staff at Arsenal Pulp Press for their continued support and vision; without you many fine queer and trans and othered voices in this country might go unheard. All my love and respect to Clyde Petersen and Rae Spoon for their talent and sparkle, and for supporting me in my return to my musical self. All my gratitude to Amber Dawn, Lidia Yuknavitch, Billeh Nickerson, Tara Hardy, Richard Van Camp, Anna Camilleri, S. Bear Bergman, and Cooper Lee Bombardier, my writing comrades and heroes both, for your words and salt and backbones and hearts and ears. I learn from you and find my own courage in our friendships. I want to thank Alison Gorman and Connie Buna for being such good brothers, and all the members of my band and butch choir for the harmony and progression.

I want to save my last and most resounding thanks for Zena Sharman, my partner, my love, my wife, my friend, and my co-conspirator. I hope to make you chicken soup and fall down laughing in our kitchen until my last breath. You make the best cheese toast. You make my life, and everything in it, shine brighter.

—IVAN E. COYOTE

Thanks to: Brian Lam, Cynara Geissler, and everyone at Arsenal Pulp Press for bringing this book to life and getting it out into the world; Ivan E. Coyote and Clyde Petersen for all of the stories, images, and performances over the past few years that make up *Gender Failure*; Claude Förster for the amazing cover image; Joëlle Rouleau, Geoff Berner, and Nolan Pike for reading the earliest versions of my pieces and offering opinions and advice; and Kendra Marks for encouraging me through every phase of writing and rewriting this book.

—RAE SPOON

Introduction

Rae Spoon and I spent the long dark month of January 2007 together in a hundred-year-old house in Dawson City, Yukon, doing an artists' residency. During our time there, we wrote a show called You Are Here, a ninety-minute live performance that blended Rae's music with my storytelling against a backdrop of projected visuals and still photographs. You Are Here was my homage to the Yukon, and small-town life in a big family; it was full of my grandmothers' wisdom, kitchen-table history, northern highways, and the midnight sun. Rae's bluegrass and country roots were a perfect musical fit for the material.

As the show came together, we realized that we were also conducting a bit of a science experiment: what could happen if a trans folk musician and a butch storyteller did a show with no specifically queer content at all? Would it increase our mainstream audience? Could we sell it to big theatres and festivals? Would it be more marketable to hide our giant homo selves and sing about universal things and tell stories about mostly straight people?

The answer to all the above turned out to be yes.

We toured *You Are Here* for five years. During that time, Rae lived for a while in Germany, and their musical interests shifted to indie rock and electronica. We both shed our cowboy shirts for tailored gingham button-downs and ties. My grandmother Florence passed away.

In the spring of 2012, Rae and I found ourselves in the green room of a big theatre in the suburbs. We had both struggled through the sound check earlier, I was about to perform memorized material told in the present tense about a grandmother whom I was mourning the passing of, Rae was tuning a banjo they hadn't played in over a year and hadn't missed, and we both had to choke back tears when the projected image of my beloved gran appeared behind us, twenty feet tall and flickering and so very deeply missed. We both knew this run was over. It had to be. We were different artists than we had been when we wrote the show, and had different things to say and sing about. We did our very best on stage that night, and received a standing ovation, and then vowed on the drive back to the hotel that that would be our last performance of *You Are Here*, and it was.

Rae told me they wanted to write a show for *us*, a show that gave us a place to talk about everything we kept to ourselves most of the time, a show that directly addressed trans issues and realities, a show that wasn't meant to make anyone comfortable or nostalgic.

"Let's write a real room-clearer of a show," Rae said in the truck in the hotel parking lot.

We shook on it.

Gender Failure was conceived that night, and born in Rae's apartment in Montreal four months later; it then grew up on stages across Canada, the US, and the UK. Rae and I vowed to push each other's performance envelopes with the project: I nudged Rae to write text and rest their hands on the fret board for more than a minute or two and tell the audience a story, and in return Rae encouraged me to sing, and to play some guitar and percussion and glockenspiel and melodica. We were both standing with one dress shoe planted firmly outside our respective comfort zones on stage. It was terrifying and at the same time opened up infinite numbers of new possibilities for both of our artistic practices.

A young and talented animator and musician by the name of Clyde Petersen saw a forty-five-minute, work-in-progress version of the show in New York in the spring of 2012, and wrote Rae a couple of days later. Clyde had been inspired by it and wanted to create some animated clips for the project. We were thrilled to have Clyde's skills and innovative hi-fi, low-tech visions on board, and our squeesome threesome was forged. Clyde set to work creating hand-drawn animations that featured two-dimensional, articulated cut-out dolls of Rae and me, which we immediately incorporated into the show, and the full shape of *Gender Failure* live performance hit the road again.

I had never worked on a project of this scope created only by trans artists before. Not having to explain or convince or defend my ideas or my reality to my fellow collaborators was a first for me. Touring with Rae and Clyde soothed me and took the lonely from the road in a way I had never experienced in quite the same way before. We watched each other's backs in rest-stop bathrooms and diners without thinking about it; it was a reflex, not a reaction. We innately understood each other because all three of us were so used to being the only one like us in the tour van.

Each time I have entered myself into the process of

envisioning and creating a significant piece of work, whether it be a novel or an album or a film or a live show, the work has changed me while I crafted it. This was even more true of *Gender Failure*.

As I finalize the edits and write this introduction, I am thinking and typing in a different body than the one I inhabited that night in the truck in the hotel parking lot.

In the spring of 2011, I finally made the decision to begin the long process of having top surgery—of having my breasts removed. I had been thinking about it for decades. I had been writing a monthly column for a national queer newspaper for over ten years, and a lot of the creative work I was producing at that time appeared initially online, which came complete with the usual unmoderated and anonymous, free-for-all comments section, full of transphobic trolls and rife with the worst examples of callousness and cruelty. As an artist and a tender heart, I had been struggling for years with the kind of nasty feedback these forums breed, and on the day I called my family doctor to begin the steps toward surgery, I made the decision that I wasn't going to write anything about this process; that this particular journey was simply too personal and possibly too painful to become fodder for public debate and discussion. The only way I could imagine mustering the bravery to begin was to tell myself that I would have surgery and heal in total privacy.

In the spring of 2012, one year after that phone call to my doctor, I tendered my resignation at the newspaper, and retired my column after eleven years. I am not convinced it was a coincidence that removing myself and my work from the torturous experience of enduring anonymous online comments as a regular part of my writing practice, and the conception of the *Gender Failure* project, happened within days of each other.

That night in my truck, when Rae and I vowed to write a show that would shine light on our true trans selves, we entered into a pact with each other to create a space together to be brave inside of, and we made a promise to place our deeply personal and individual truths on the dashboard as our compass.

We kept that promise to each other, and then along the way picked up Clyde standing next to a freeway onramp somewhere, and now here we all are.

Creating this book has changed me. Working on it with Rae and Clyde helped me to become the person I needed to be, and inhabit the body I needed to be in, and for that immense and profound gift, I will forever be grateful to both of them.

As I am also thankful for you, the reader, for picking this book up and turning its pages.

Introduction

I was assigned female at birth and socialized as a girl in a Pentecostal family in Calgary, Alberta. My attempts at being a girl failed epically throughout my teenage years, but I had never considered that it was something that I would be allowed to change. I had no way to talk about gender. I wasn't allowed to express how uncomfortable it was for me. To resist would have put me in danger, so I kept any subversive thoughts covert. As a person who couldn't conform to what was expected of me, I thought I was a failure and kept it to myself.

I came out as transgender privately in the summer of 2001, and publicly in 2002. I knew that identifying as a man and asking to be called "he" would be difficult in relation to the outside world, and I wasn't wrong. Even more difficult was that, as a male-identified person, I didn't feel allowed to discuss the parts of that side of the gender binary that were problematic to me. I felt a dysphoria in my new trans-identity and I thought it must be another failure on my part.

When I retired from gender, it was because I came to the realization that the gender binary was what had been failing me all along. It's hard to imagine that any one person finds that their place in the binary fits them without some measure of discomfort. Since my "retirement," I have been striving to stop gendering things for myself and for other people.

Ivan Coyote is a great friend and long-time collaborator of mine. In the past, we worked together on a show about the Yukon, which was more focused on stories about place than our own identities. Through the process of touring that first show, we discovered a lot of similarities between us due to our non-binary genders, so we started bonding organically over small-town gas stations, public washrooms, and the general lack of understanding in the world in which we moved.

In the spring of 2012, a few months after I came out as gender-retired, Ivan and I wrote our first version of the show *Gender Failure*. We presented it in New York at Dixon Place. The reception we got from that first show alone made it clear that we were on to something. Bringing together the stories inspired by the show in this book is the best way I can think of to include everything that we don't have time to present during the course of a ninety-minute performance. Visual artist and musician Clyde Petersen was in the audience for that first show and was inspired to collaborate with us and create accompanying animations, which we premiered as part of our performance in March 2013 at the London Lesbian and Gay Film Festival in London, England. The enthusiastic feedback we received confirmed that we had found an irreplaceable artistic partner in Clyde.

I have been failing at the gender binary for as long as I can remember, and that has been difficult at every level of my life. I constantly find myself explaining how this happened on a daily basis, whether to people I meet or to the media. This book is my attempt to trace my journey with gender; it's a group of life stories and personal essays meant to express how I have felt throughout my life in my various identities. Although I belong to a gender minority, I am a white, able-bodied, gender-neutral (formerly trans-masculine) person, and I recognize that there are many ways that I benefit from privilege, especially in queer spaces. There should be as many books like this as there are people constrained by the gender binary, and I hope in my lifetime to read as many of them as possible.

Girl Failure

Janine Jones and I were best friends from grade two until grade eight. We bonded on the day during crafts time when someone took a straw and blew a tiny glass bead straight into Jennifer McCloud's ear, and she had to go to emergency. Our teacher, Miss McCarthy, went with her, so the principal came in to supervise the class. He stood at the front of the room and bellowed that the right thing to do was for whoever had blown the bead to be a man, step forward, and admit what he had done. But both Janine and I had seen that it was Carrie Halliday, a girl bigger than most of the boys, who had been the actual bead blower. Carrie Halliday was famous for having had to repeat grade one already, and she was mean, prone to unprovoked snakebites and knuckle punches and shin kicks, so neither one of us said a word, because like all of us, including Miss McCarthy, we were terrified of Carrie Halliday. Janine smiled down at her desk and then her gaze slipped sideways across the aisle and met mine. We both raised our eyebrows in acknowledgment of the truth and nodded. We were complicit in the secret, silent partners in someone else's crime, and that was all it took.

Three weeks later, behind the baseball diamond, Janine and I stabbed our pinkie fingers with a safety pin we had scorched with a match and declared each other blood brothers forever.

I lived on Hemlock Street, one block away by street and one minute away by footpath through the greenbelt from Janine's parents' house on Poplar Street. It turned out that we both liked sports and camping and that book *The Chrysalids*; neither of us went in for Barbies or playing house or had any interest in doing our hair or stuff like that.

Janine Jones and I were inseparable for those years; I ate dinner at her place two or three nights a week, and we were always sleeping over at each other's houses. We were like sisters, people said, which always made me snort a little, because my real sister and I could hardly stand to be in the same room together for five minutes without tearing holes in each other, metaphorically or otherwise. And Janine only had two brothers, both of whom were pretty much useless, Gerome being a chronic masturbator at home and a science nerd at school, and little Marcus being a bit of a bed wetter and still needing us to babysit him so he wouldn't play with matches or the stove or a propane curling iron again, or catch his foreskin in his zipper as he was prone to doing due to his unexplained aversion to wearing underwear. Marcus was our responsibility, not our comrade.

Anyway, we were better than sisters, until the start of grade eight when they finally finished that new junior high school on Hickory Street, and for some reason Janine signed up for home economics class instead of shop like we had planned to, and it turned out it was because home-ec was what Jeanie and Sandra and Wendy and Tracey and Kerri-Anne and tall Rebecca were taking, and she was into hanging out with them more, ever since they all went horseback riding together at the summer barbecue for Janine's mom's work. Who knew all their moms worked together at the Department of Motor Vehicles office? What a coincidence.

Next thing I know, Janine is bra shopping with all of them, and I am not invited because I don't even need or want a training bra yet. So I guess the first things that ever truly came between the two of us were those breasts. They set us apart; how could they not?

It seemed to me that those breasts of hers had appeared kind of overnight the summer after grade six, and they were a C cup, easy, by the time we hit the new junior high. Of course there were the grade nine boys there, the older boys, and of course they noticed, and come to think of it, that was the second thing that would eventually split us up: those boys. The third thing was cheerleading. *Oh Mickey you're so fine you're so fine you blow my mind hey Mickey. Hey Mickey.* There was no way I could dance to that or shake any pom-poms; just the thought of moving my hips in front of anyone much less a crowd made me freeze ice cold blood in my ears but Janine was so into it and even liked the skirt that came with it. Who was this new girl, anyway? And what had she done with my friend who only liked blue jeans or brown cords, just like me?

The fourth and final element of our undoing was the slumber party. Every birthday for six years before that one of hers in the fall of grade eight had been the same: our moms would rent us a couple of movies and buy a bucket of Kentucky Fried Chicken for dinner. But not the fall of 1983. That year Janine decided she was having a slumber party and that all of her new friends from horseback riding and home-ec and cheerleading were coming too. We had Chinese food instead of fried chicken because the cheerleaders wouldn't eat fried foods, and we watched *Pretty in Pink* instead of Monty Python, and I fell asleep early because I was tired from playing that day in a boys' hockey tournament, which everyone also thought was weird.

I was curled up in my Smokey the Bear sleeping bag in one corner of the rec room near the electric piano and woke up some time in the wee hours of the night. I must have heard my name being spoken in my sleep because they were all talking about me. Wendy, Tracy, Sandra, Jeanie, Kerri-Anne, tall Rebecca, and worst thing ever, my best friend Janine too, talking about me, and laughing at my flat and training-braless chest and hairless armpits. I could feel my dinner churn in my stomach and burn in the back of my throat like I had drank battery acid, and the tears welled and fell and rolled, rolled, I could not control them at all. And then it got so much worse.

My best friend's voice hiccupped, it was all just so hilarious, and hopped over a giggle when she told the rest of the girls that I had no hair down there yet either; bald as an egg, she said. "And you should see her thing. Her, *you know*. It is huge. As long as half my pointer finger, seriously, and it hangs right down past her lips and looks just like a tiny you-know-what."

"How sick!" someone said, then another peal of laughter, another voice, it sounded like Wendy, and I pictured her talking through her retainer and headgear; she wasn't so perfect, either. Then I heard the swish of her, so weak from laughing at me, that she fell backwards into her dad's down sleeping bag.

The last time I ever took my clothes off in the open space of a women's change room, I was thirteen years old and had just started grade eight at a new school. To this day, when in strange gyms, I still change in a bathroom stall, and I have a scar on my elbow where I split it open on the rough edge of a toilet paper dispenser to prove it.

Janine and I didn't hang out much after that night, and we never talked about why. She lives in Manitoba now, and runs a pizza restaurant with her husband and two kids. Still plays the flute and does a little theatre. Every once in a while she will drunk dial me on a Friday night and tell me she is an artist too, you know, that she is writing down some stories about when we were kids. I never ask her if she knows or writes about why our friendship fell apart. It was partly those breasts and partly those boys and partly that home-ec class, but for me it was mostly the way she talked about my little dick that night in the rec room in the half basement of her parents' house on Poplar Street. I have been carrying that night with me for thirty years, and just now was the first time I ever put it down. Put it down in words.

Girl Failure

For the first nineteen years of my life, my gender was a like an amusement park ride that I couldn't escape from. My mother often told me that I looked like a tiny doll when I was born. She'd say, "You didn't have any dents on your head like the other babies. You had a full head of hair, and the nurses would fight over who got to hold you. Such a beautiful baby girl! Must have been because I have strong stomach muscles." She would say this while patting herself on the belly.

Being a girl was something that never really happened for me. The first day of junior high gym class, I was horrified when I realized that we were going to have to change our clothes in a locker room. The other girls collected near the rows of beige-coloured lockers and talked about shaving their legs. I dodged into a bathroom stall. I could hear them all singing a song together as I hid, pulling my t-shirt over my head. I think the song was "I Will Always Love You." *How do they all know the same song?* I thought. My Pentecostal parents had only ever let me listen to Christian music.

During gymnastics that day, I was on the parallel bars trying to hold myself up when I felt a hot ripping pain in my chest. My arms gave out. I started crying, crumpled up on the floor. The gym teacher came over and said, "You're okay. You're not hurt," and pulled me up to my feet. I could feel my face turn red. One of the other girls came up to me with a wide grin and said, "Hey, it's okay. I used to want to be a boy too." I felt the floor giving way beneath me. This was the second time she'd gone out of her way to point out that I was bad at being a girl. She was on to me.

A week later, we moved into the dance aerobics portion of gym class. The boys were outside playing rugby, which looked violent, but not as dangerous as moving around to dance music. I had never been allowed to dance in my life. My parents thought it was sinful. When the pumping beat of "Rhythm Is a Dancer" came on, the gym teacher started to call out moves and demonstrate them, which we were supposed to follow. I could feel my body resisting as I urged it to move to the music like a limp scarecrow. I knew that if I didn't dance, I'd be in trouble, but if I did, I might go to hell. I thought I saw the gym teacher raise her eyebrow at me as I shimmied robotically behind all the girls who seemed to be genuinely enjoying the experience. At the end of the class, the gym teacher said, "Good job, girls! Tomorrow you'll break up into groups and come up with your own routines."

That night while I was in the bathtub, I looked at my mom's pink razor. I grabbed it and turned it over in my hand. I could still hear the girls in the locker room that day talking about shaving. I had to do something. I dragged the razor up my leg, slicing off the tiny blond hairs. But then I slipped and cut my knee. Blood dripped into the bath water. *Can't stop now*, I thought. I bit my lip and continued. Afterwards my mother saw my legs covered in cuts. "What happened to you?" she asked.

28

I hung my head. "I shaved my legs."

"But you're only twelve," she said. "You don't need to."

"Yes, I do!" I said. She didn't know how much I needed to do something that made me seem like a girl.

"Well, did you use soap? Next time, use soap." She patted my head and walked away.

In gym class the next day, no one noticed my attempts at becoming a woman. The teacher broke us into groups. "Come up with a routine to the song I give you," she instructed. Our group was assigned "Gonna Make You Sweat (Everybody Dance Now)." I had never heard the song before. We took our tiny stereo and went to a corner of the gymnasium.

"We should start in a line," one girl said, trying to take control, "and then we can wave our arms up and down like this. It will look like water!"

Kill me now, I thought.

Slowly our gymnastic routine unfolded. It involved a lot of loosely choreographed manoeuvres that we tried to do in unison. We made the routine longer by doing our moves close to each other, and then further apart. By the end of the class, I was certain that we had created a performance that would not only confirm how deeply flawed I was at being a girl, but also send me straight to hell, forever.

The next day was showtime. One by one, groups went up and managed to perform their routines through waves of giggles. Suddenly it was our turn. I stood up and joined my group on the blue gym mat. My heart was racing. The gym teacher pressed play on our song and we stood motionless in a line, waiting for the right note to kick in before starting the routine. As the synthesizers washed over us, though, something happened to me. Something far back in my mind snapped. *I can't do this*, I thought. From some distant part of my psyche, one word came to me: *Run.*

I bolted out of the line and out of the gym like someone had pulled a pin out of a grenade. By the time the lead singer had started, I was halfway down the hallway. I was inside a school in the far reaches of suburban Calgary, surrounded by neighbourhoods with schools exactly like it. I had no idea where I was running to.

Ghost of a Boy

E   Abmin   A
Ghost of a Boy.

E   Abmin   A
Hard to catch like light.

E   Abmin   A
I'll hide you in my body.

E   Abmin A
I'll keep you alive.

Ooh
Ooh
Ooh
Ooh

Ghost of a Boy.
Hard to catch like light.
I'll hide you in my body.
I'll keep you alive.

*O*lder butch sightings in airports make me feel like I am part of an army. A quiet, button-down, peacekeeping brigade that nods instead of saluting. Silver hair and eye wrinkles are earned instead of stripes or medals.

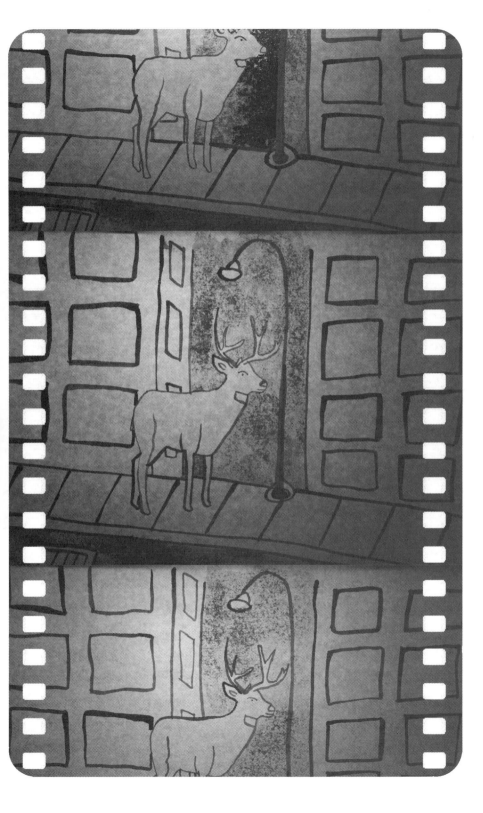

Rosie

I was nineteen, almost twenty, when I first met Rosie. I still had long hair when I met her; that's how many ages ago it was.

I was living in Vancouver's West End, still wet behind the ears, having just arrived from the Yukon in a Volkswagen van. It was only the second apartment I ever rented, and the first time I laid eyes on Rosie it was raining, and there she was, skinny, wiry, restless-eyed Rosie right behind me on the sidewalk that led to our building's front door with both of her arms burdened down with grocery bags. So I held the door open for her, just like my gran had taught me to.

"Chivalry lives," she snorted as she clunked in past me in her skin-tight Levi's and low-cut blouse and kitten heels. Of course, I did not know the words for kitten heels. Yet.

Except her voice was low, like an eighteen-wheeler gearing down with its engine brakes grinding on a long steep hill down from the summit, and her bare skin above her black bra was covered in five o'clock shadow and painted with now bleeding-edged and sailor-flash faded tattoos.

I had never met any other woman quite like Rosie before.

Still haven't, really. I tried chatting her up in the laundry room a couple of times after that, but she ignored me like she hadn't heard me speak at all. Made me think of the she-wolves back home in the Yukon, at Danny Nolan's game farm on the hotsprings road. You could tell those wolves wanted to come up and sniff your palms and lick your fingers and take a bit of moose meat or a bone from you, but the wildness still inside them wouldn't allow themselves that kind of trust, that kind of closeness to a possible enemy just acting like it was a friend. Those she-wolves, they would go without meat, just so as not to be disappointed by a stranger's ill intent again, and Rosie, she made me remember those she-wolves, she sure did.

It took me months, slowly, slowly, to get her to smile, and then chat, and then one day, accept my third or fourth invitation to come in for a cup of tea. I referred to her as "he" only once, early on, I didn't know, I was still so small-town back then. I used the word "he" for her only once and it was barely out of my mouth when she caught it in one manicured and muscled fist and tossed it back at me. She wasn't mad, just certain. "Don't ever call me 'he,'" she said calmly. "Ever. I hate it. I am a she. Her. Hers. Got it, kid?"

Seemed simple to me. And it is. I loved her already. I wanted to make her happy. Call her what she wanted. Call her what made her happy to hear.

Somewhere in there, she took to calling me Luigi. I don't remember why. Luigi the bricklayer, even though I was working as a landscaper at the time. We would garbolocize at night after work, garbolocize she called it, a word she had made up, meaning I would drive my van up and down the alleys behind rich people's houses and she would smoke her hand-rolled cigarettes with the sliding door open and look for antiques and other quality stuff that the rich people discarded. You wouldn't believe what people would put out with the trash back then. Rosie had a one-bedroom, same as me, but she slept on a pull-out in the living room with her bird and her plants and her cat Miss Puss, so the bedroom could be used as a shop. We stripped those antiques down and refinished them with love and sweat and fancy carpenter's wax, old school ways, she taught me, oak and teak and bird's eye maple even, one time we found a radio cabinet with a phonograph and everything worked perfect and we shined that sweetheart up and sold it right back to the rich folks in an antique store not a block away from where we got it.

I mostly bought weed and t-shirts with my profits, but Rosie was saving up for her surgeries and electrolysis. She hated the electrolysis, called it the never-ending story. She would come home after with her eyes rimmed red from crying. And she called me Luigi, and he, and I never asked her why. Didn't need to. It made me happy.

One day after about ten months of us being friends like that, eating dinners that we cooked for each other and listening to Nina Simone until I would cry and she would laugh at me and punch me in the arm because both of us avoided hugging anyone back then as best we could, my friend Archie came to town for a visit. Archie the fag from Red Deer, Alberta, a chef and a fellow tinker and traveller. He slept on my couch for five days or so, and put out his Camels unfiltered in the houseplant Rosie had given me, and left his smelly, crusty socks around and the seat up and was generally pissing me off and overstaying his welcome, but I still loved him, and he told great stories, Archie did, but anyways what happened was Rosie came down one night with some homemade baked beans for me with the bacon cooked right in because she knew they were my favourite. She hung around in the doorway, too shy to enter with

Archie the stranger sprawled out on the couch behind me. She was even whispering.

"It's cool," I told her. "He's my friend. Come on in, I'll make you some tea. I missed you these last couple of days. Archie is cool. He's gay himself."

"Gay has nothing to do with being cool at all," she said, hissing a little, and she came in and drank a cup of tea, but didn't stay for long.

And Archie was cool. Enough, I guess. He called her Rosie in a weird way, though, said her name like it was in quotation marks, kind of, hard to describe but I remember hoping she couldn't hear it in his voice since she didn't know him. Maybe he just said everybody's name like he didn't quite believe that they were who they said they were?

After Rosie left too soon, Archie lit a smoke and grinned mean and big. "That was the ugliest drag queen I have ever seen in my life," he said. "And I thought I had seen it all. Girlfriend, give it up already. Who does she think she's fooling?"

I remember the feeling of hating someone I loved at that moment. I had felt it before but only with my blood family. Hating Archie and his ten-percent spandex t-shirts and his Docksider shoes with no socks and his callous heart and how could he talk like that about Rosie when he should know better, since he was gay from Alberta. And I was the one who said he could be trusted, so he made me a liar by accident.

That three-storey apartment building was sold a couple months later and torn down to build a high-rise. Rosie ended up in a single room occupancy hotel on Cordova Street, and was diagnosed with terminal stomach cancer at the end of that summer. Her doctor told her she was going to have to go off her hormones and take care of her real medical condition, but she told me on the phone that she wasn't going to do it. She asked a neighbour to cat-sit Miss Puss for the weekend, left him with every can of cat food she could get her hands on, and disappeared. Her friend Rachel and I opened up a missing persons case for her after the front desk guy at the hotel she was staying at called us and said we were the only two numbers she had written down and left on the bedside table before she up and bailed out on him and did we want to come and get her stuff then? "Some old tools mostly," he said. He must have liked her. He didn't have to do that, and most guys like that wouldn't have. I still have some of Rosie's tools; they were in my garage when my house burned down and so they have survived, just like I sometimes dream Rosie did, too. Sometimes I catch a glimpse of the shape of her or see a footstep that looks like the way she walked in someone else on a sidewalk some days and my heart skips, but it always stills quickly. I know Rosie is dead. She wasn't for a while when she was first gone, but she is now, I can feel it. I still remember everything I learned from Rosie. She taught me how to take something some people might just throw out, and then sweat and work and love it back to beautiful.

Joan

Capo on 2

Chorus:
Joan. I love you Joan. (G)
Don't walk home all alone. (Am) (D) (G)

They put on their orange (G)
They get in their trucks (Am)
They load their shot guns (C)
and drive down to main street. (D) (G)

They look out their windows
like it's the edge of a highway
and we're a kind of wild
they don't understand

hunting, hunting, hunting (C) (D) (G) (Em)
hunting both of us. (C) (D) (G)

         Chorus

We're a kind of wild
They don't understand
because we're not obligated
to be a woman or a man.

But we are stronger together
we won't hide when we're hunted
let's walk home
holding hands.

         Chorus

let's walk home together
      alone.

CANADA

PAR AVION
VIA AIR MAIL

God Failure

On the day of my dedication, when I was slated to meet Jesus for the first time, I was only a couple of months old. There is a photo of me sitting askew on my uncle Carl's lap, and he has a huge grin beneath his handlebar moustache. He was holding me until my parents were ready to take me up to the front of the church. Apparently the pink satin dress my mother had put me in turned out to be a hazard, and I was as slippery as a little frog in his hands.

I would often see that photo of myself when, as a child, I flipped through my baby book with my mother. "Uncle Carl said he almost dropped you ten times," my mother would add to the story between laughs. "He was scared he would break you. Luckily, we still got you up to the front of the church to give you to Jesus."

A dedication is the moment when the parents of a new-born baby pledge to raise it Christian, along with everything that comes with it: in my case, being a girl in a tradition that still separated genders and gender roles along a strict divide. I wonder what would have happened if Uncle Carl had just let me go to where I was sliding? Would I have slithered to gender retirement in the north of Montreal, where I live now? Or chosen the long way through all of the years of trying to be a girl and then a man before retiring from gender completely? Most likely I would have lain on the floor feeling abandoned and crying until he picked me up again. There isn't a lot of choice when you're an infant.

There wasn't a lot of choice in cleaning a toilet as a nine-year-old, either. After my mother told me it was going to be part of my weekly chore routine, I knew that I could stay in that bathroom for as long as I wanted, but the only way out was to learn how to make the porcelain sink and toilet glisten. I cleaned them as fast as possible so I could go outside and play road hockey with my brother. In our house, it was only the girls who had to clean. At first I thought it was based on age because my sister and I were older, but as both of my brothers' ninth birthdays came and went, I noticed that they hadn't been inducted into the world of household chores like we had. It made no sense to me. The boys used the toilet as much as we did and, as I had observed in my weekly cleaning missions, made more of a mess of it. As soon as I could reach into the kitchen sink, washing the dinner dishes was added to my list of chores. I could see where this was going. Soon we would be doing everything for the men around us—just like our mother.

Instead of thinking too much about my impending womanhood, I often ran to a ravine located on the hill above our house, the only place nearby that was covered in trees. I would run through it at full speed by myself, often picking up a stick to use as a sword so I could battle invisible opponents or take whacks at the underbrush. I would pick through the burnt remains of beer cans and cigarette butts in the cold ashes of the covert fires that teenagers had partied around on the weekend. I craved the unbridled freedom of acting how I wanted. Hot blood would rush through my body. I felt lighter the more I ran. I would go there to throw *it* off. I knew that *it* was something I was bad at, that I had to try at. *It* followed me wherever there were eyes to notice. Soon, though, I was back at the dinner table praying over a meal and being told that someday I would be someone's wife. Growing up felt like a waterfall that was far off in the distance but unavoidable because I could never pull myself out of the water. The current was too strong. I didn't want to grow up to be a woman where everyone could see me. I wanted to live in a ravine, in a tree fort by myself.

Fast forward to a Sunday service at a Pentecostal church in northwest Calgary. I'm thirteen years old. I'm wearing army boots, a white blouse, and a black peasant skirt covered in flowers. It falls just above my ankles when I'm standing, swishing above my feet as I walk into church with my family. Two parents, two girls, two boys. We look like a perfect and planned balance. We sit in no real order in the pew, except for my parents, who are in the middle next to each other with children of various heights and genders on either side of them. The sermon starts and we sit up straight with our hands in our laps, trying to concentrate on staring straight ahead. After fifteen minutes I'm like a cowboy straddling a fence. My legs are spread wide apart because I want to be comfortable for the long wait. There is no real end time to a Pentecostal service. I've loaded my patch-work purple and teal leather purse with things to do: tiny notebooks, black pens, mints in wrappers. My mother hears me unwrap a mint surreptitiously, the crinkling paper for a moment eclipsing the sound of the pastor's excited voice. She looks down the pew toward us. She sees my legs open and I can feel her glare upon me. I'm too old for her to take me to the church washroom for a spanking, so she just motions to me with her head. I look down and correct myself.

This was female socialization in our family. I acted how I felt most naturally, and I was corrected, over and over again, until I learned not to act on my impulses, even though I still felt them. The thing about failing as a girl is that I did want to succeed. I wanted to be liked and accepted like anyone, but it wasn't like learning how to play the guitar or to roller-blade. It was something that was always just out of my reach, something I could never really learn to do well, no matter how much I practiced.

Being a girl was complicated enough before I started dating, but the other girls in the church youth group had a giddiness when they talked about boys that I didn't feel, or even really understand. I wanted in on whatever they were feeling, even though I didn't feel very giddy about anything. I hadn't had any elementary school boyfriends, or been invited to any parties where I might have gotten one in junior high. Youth group was really my only chance at popularity or a boyfriend, and I wanted to see what dating was all about. When I was fourteen, I met a boy named Chad there who had a diamond stud earring and who pretended he could play the guitar. His mother had been one of the leaders of the Christian girls' club I had gone to every Wednesday when I was younger. One night at youth group, I sat playing guitar in a small hallway off the main room. He walked up to me, sat down, and wiped his hands on his pants. Then he took my hand into his cold and sweaty palm, looked into my eyes, and asked me if I would be his girlfriend. Completely surprised by the attention, I managed to say yes. We then spent most of our time together jumping to the Kris Kross song "Jump," making each other guitar pick necklaces, skateboarding, and holding hands during Sunday services. I was starting to feel like I was getting the hang of growing up after all.

A few weeks after we started dating, the youth pastor gave a sermon about how marriage was supposed to be something that honoured the name of God: one man and one woman. He explained that in the union of a marriage, a woman's body goes back to the man's, as Eve was made out of Adam's rib. He said there was nothing more peaceful or godly than obeying the laws of the Bible in holy matrimony. The whole time he preached, I was stealing looks at Chad. So far we hadn't kissed because I'd been avoiding it. The idea of it didn't seem as fun as everything else we were doing, like skateboarding.

Then the youth pastor began to address the boys. "Men are the spiritual leaders of a household," he proclaimed. "They rule over all the members of their households. A man is responsible for his wife and children."

I shot a direct look at Chad. He was slouching low in his seat, wearing torn jeans and a "No Fear" t-shirt, with his hands in his pockets. *If I kept dating Chad and someday we kissed and even got married, he would be the lord over me?* It seemed like a bad deal. He was a lot worse at the guitar than I was, and I was already having to pretend he was better at music than he really was. What would I get out of cleaning the house and cooking for him every day? My experiment in dating started to feel dangerous. Soon it cooled off and ended because I refused to kiss him, and he told me that he had kissed someone else. I was fine with it.

It was for girls that I felt the giddiness that I was supposed to feel for boys. I had crushes on so many girls in junior high and high school, with their hairsprayed bangs and Gap perfume. I would think about those girls as I walked through the mall with my mother. I was supposed to be shopping, but suddenly

I would be hit by a waft of perfume that I had longed for all day in class. When I finally decided to make a break for it and defy the church and all of its hellfire teachings, I discovered the things that I thought I just didn't have in me, like the way my heart would take off when I finally held hands with, and then kissed, a girl.

I came out to my friends slowly. Only a handful of them were uncomfortable about it and ditched me. Once I had a girlfriend, it finally made sense to me that I hadn't really wanted a boyfriend. I thought I must have just always been gay. Since I had no homosexual role models, I started to covertly read lesbian magazines that I got from a magazine store downtown to discover exactly how being gay was supposed to work. The magazines didn't contain a lot of clues, just articles about Ellen, Sandra Bernhard, and the Indigo Girls. None of these lesbians seemed very close to who I was, though. Maybe I would understand better when I was old enough to meet other gay people.

One thing I was certain of was that I had strayed far from where my parents had wanted their god to take me when they dedicated my life to him. My inability to act like a girl without intense effort, combined with my attraction to other girls, was subject to condemnation, but for me there wasn't a choice. I have been to many churches and met many Christians who accept people like me and still believe in God, but the resistance I experienced as I fled burned all the bridges between me and him. For me, Jesus is now more like my ex-boyfriend Chad: someone I knew well, but don't think about a lot anymore.

Listing My Sisters

November 19, 2012

As I write this, I am sitting in my nearly vacant office on campus at a university where I am the writer-in-residence for this semester. Nothing but a desk, a corkboard empty except for a handful of the previous tenant's thumbtacks, and me. A woman just left my office after a brief meeting, and right after she was gone I let out a deep breath, and started to type.

Tomorrow is the Trans Day of Remembrance. That young woman had come to ask me if I had any names of fallen trans people I wished to be included during the vigil tomorrow night.

Where would I start? Do I start with the artist I once knew back in the day, how she played the violin, too, and how she took her own life after years of struggling with depression? What I remember is that the final straw for her was auditioning to play a dead body in a dumpster on one of those police procedural television shows that was being shot in town. She had been asked to audition for the part of a dead trans woman, but it had been given to a cisgendered female actor.

The director thought the cisgendered actor would be "more believable."

The Trans Day of Remembrance will be the only day set aside in this school year on this campus to specifically honour or recognize trans people. It is not a celebration, rather, it is a solemn affair during which participants will gather to read a list of our fallen. Our murdered. Those of us who died from suicide or AIDS-related illness, or overdose or poverty or hatred and ignorance and racism. Or all of the above.

Someone will wheel a couple of speakers into a common area on campus somewhere, and a microphone will be set up. This is Canada, and the students here are generally a fairly well-heeled lot, so what I am expecting will happen is that a few activist students, probably white and mostly middle-class, some queer and some genderqueer and some trans, though most probably trans masculine, will read out a list of names to remember. Most names will belong to trans women, many women of colour, some of whom were sex workers, and many of whom were either born poor or died poor. There will be little or no analysis presented as to who these trans people were, or why the dead are mostly trans women and the living people reading their names aloud are often not.

What will be missing are these women's stories. Their triumphs and talents and tribulations. We will be reminded only of their names. Most of the queer students will resume classes afterwards, and go to pride dances and Coming Out Day celebrations, and not think much about this list of names again until next year, because, really, trans women's issues and realities don't affect them all that much. The trans masculine folks will still be allowed, even welcomed, into women's spaces, radical queer sex parties, women's music festivals, and women's studies programs at exclusive colleges and universities. And living trans women or trans-feminine people will continue to be excluded from some transition homes and shelters, some music festivals, some women's spaces, a lot of lesbian feminist bedrooms, most dyke erotica and pornography, and nearly all of the good parties. What will also be missing is a discussion about the difference between excluding someone and actively including them, and intentionally making space. And the day after we are supposed to remember, most of this will be forgotten.

Tomorrow I will remember my friend Rosie. All of her. How, if she were here, she would have stood at the back of the crowd, smoking and making wisecracks. How someone would have probably turned around and shushed her for talking too loud during her own candlelight vigil.

Rosie disappeared, never to be seen from again, over twenty years ago now, shortly after being diagnosed with terminal cancer. She had been told by her doctor that he could no longer ethically prescribe hormones to her, as he suspected that long-term heavy estrogen use while she saved up money for the many surgeries that at that time were not covered by our province's health care plan had been a contributing factor to the tumours growing in her stomach and intestines. He had recommended that she cease her use of female hormones and concentrate on her, and I quote, "real and more pressing medical concerns."

Rosie had disagreed. She packed up one suitcase, socked away all the remaining hormones she had been stockpiling, and vanished. None of us ever saw her again. She never was much for long goodbyes. It was common knowledge at the time that you could buy hormones on the black market south of the border, and we all assumed that was where she had gone. And now, given that it is twenty-three years after her then terminal diagnosis, and given that I never heard a single word from her or about her since, I am forced to assume that she is dead.

But I refuse to reduce her life to nothing more than a name on a list of the deceased. I want all of who she was to be remembered, to be honoured. I want it to be known that Rosie's life also contained joy, and laughter and friendship and love, in addition to despair and poverty and cancer and death.

Because you cannot fight despair armed only with more despair.

So. I will remember so much more about Rosie than just her absence from my life. I can tell you that Rosie loved to build little dollhouses, those fancy ones with real wood floors and fireplaces made from tiny bricks and roofs of miniature shingles that she glued into place one by one with tweezers, squinting over her bifocals. She had a cat named Miss Puss and a parakeet who couldn't sing that she nicknamed Madonna but whose actual name was Lynda Carter, the actress who played Wonder Woman, and she owned over one hundred houseplants, which she watered at the crack of dawn every morning wearing her infamous high-heeled shoes. I know for sure about this part because I was her downstairs neighbour, and some days it sounded like she was learning to tap dance upstairs on top of my head.

One time, a guy tried to assault her in an alley when she was walking home in those very same heels after getting us bagels at the bakery around the corner. He tried to grab her black leather purse, but Rosie, she used to box when she was in the navy, and she ended up kicking his ass. Finished him off with a knee to the face and knocked out two of his teeth. She arrived at my door still breathless, but recounted the incident like she was describing a fight in a hockey game that she had just seen the highlights of on the six o'clock news, not like something that had happened to her in real life just minutes earlier.

When I brought her a glass of water and asked her if she was okay, she just shrugged. "Okay enough," she growled, "except that fucker owes me a new pair of tights. Must have been his teeth that tore a hole right through the knee, here, look." She pulled up her denim skirt to show me. "Brand new pair, too. Like money grows on trees, right? He won't be trying that manoeuvre again any time soon."

Rosie made the best baked beans ever, right from scratch, and taught me how to refinish furniture. That was how she saved money for electrolysis and her many surgeries; she salvaged pieces of discarded furniture from alleys and curbs all around the city and brought them back to high-gloss life. She collected bone china teacups with matching saucers from yard sales and thrift stores and kept them in a bird's eye maple cabinet and only brought them out for special occasions or Really Bad Days. She hated being hugged, but every once in a while she would touch my hair or my cheek soft as could be with one of her gnarly ex-sailor's hands, then pull away as soon as I acknowledged the fact she was touching me, like my head was a burner on the stove she had forgotten she had left on.

What else? She was a foster kid originally from Quebec, but not even I could get her to talk about her childhood much, ever. She was Métis, but she didn't speak much about that, either. She once shook hands with Pierre Elliott Trudeau. She could talk with a lit cigarette dangling from her pursed lips while she fixed her hair or fried eggs or sanded a teak sideboard better than anyone I have ever met, including my father. The smoke would curl up in swirling blue fingers and into her eyes and long bangs, but she never blinked. She rolled her own, with those little tubes and the machine and the tobacco that came in a tin. She wore too-loose false teeth that clicked sometimes when she laughed too deep and she would knuckle-punch you hard in the upper arm if you even brought it up. She never missed an episode of "The Young and the Restless," but she would kill me dead if she knew I told anyone that.

I will remember all of what she showed me of her life, and how she lived it. Her death is almost surely a fact, an unsubstantiated but statistically unavoidable probability. I will mourn her death, of course, but it seems more important to me that I celebrate her life, and cherish what she brought into mine. I will never forget her. I will remember all I can of my friend Rosie.

And then I will work to never forget my living trans sisters. I will speak their names aloud, too, and then get to work. Work to earn the word "brother."

Cowboy

Every Calgary Stampede, the city is a sea of brand new white cowboy hats and denim worn by office workers who have probably never been on a farm. You can see them in the evening, sauntering around drunk from office parties with little bits of straw stuck to their outfits from the bales of hay that are trucked downtown for the events. I grew up in the suburbs. My father was one of those office workers. I never lived in the country as a child, but my mother's family is different.

I could always tell that my uncle Carl was at my grandma's house by his worn brown cowboy boots at the door. They stood up straight as if his legs were still in them. Uncle Carl lived with his wife and two sons in a mobile home out in the country. Every once in a while they would decide to move and bring their mobile home with them. I remember being amazed that we could pull up to the same house in a completely new location. When we walked inside, everything was just the same. It was like a spaceship that could take off and then land somewhere else.

Uncle Carl loved horses. He rode them until he was bow-legged. I would watch him amble around and think about how the horses had changed the shape of his legs to fit their bodies. Sometimes he would take his own horse out for us to ride. He would lift my sister and me up onto it and then lead us around slowly. I felt so tall on top and safe with my uncle holding the reins.

Uncle Carl has worked the oil rigs for as long as I can remember. We would never know if he was going to show up at Christmas or Thanksgiving until that day. It all depended on whether his boss gave the crew the time off or not, and that depended on the price of crude oil. Sometimes he would drive twelve hours straight back from Saskatchewan to be with us. Other times he would be unreachable, working somewhere out on the flat, frozen land. One Christmas when he came home, he hadn't told anyone that he had lost part of a finger a few months earlier, and he made a practical joke out of it. He came up to me and did the trick where he pretended to pull part of his finger off, which is usually done by tucking the finger back and making part of the thumb on the other hand look like it was the detached part of the finger. This time there was no "just kidding" part at the end, and he laughed for half an hour after I shrieked when I discovered that there was indeed a part of his finger missing. But I loved it when he paid attention to me even if he sometimes shocked me. I didn't even have any bad feelings for him after he accidentally dislocated my arm when he was trying to put me on his shoulders; I just cried until my relatives gave me candy and then we found out that my arm had popped itself back into its socket on the trip to the emergency room.

My uncles who work the oil rigs are often away from home for months at a time. They work fourteen-hour days or more

through every season that the prairies throw at them. All three of them dropped out of high school as soon as they could, but now they earn more money than a lot of people who went to university. Life on the oil rigs is lonely. When I was a child, it was not unusual to get a drunken call from one of my uncles in the middle of the night, wanting to talk to all four of us kids and tell us that he loved us. We would make jokes about it and warn each other as we passed the receiver, but I felt my uncles' isolation and identified with it.

When my brother Jack died, they were his pallbearers. They carried his coffin without crying from the church to the hearse. I looked up at them when they passed by me and hoped to be strong like them. When my schizophrenic father would fly off the handle, at least one of them would always show up to protect us. My father was scared of them and would take off as soon as one showed up in a truck. They made him look like a tiny guy in a white shirt and thick tie because they were real cowboys. I needed to see that there were people who were un- afraid of him in order to get over my own fear.

Sometimes, in daydreams, I pictured myself as one of them, out in the middle of the prairies driving alone in my truck, blowing smoke out the window, and sleeping in hotels and temporary trailers. I would listen to Garth Brooks, Willie Nelson, and Randy Travis. My hands would be dirty with crude oil. I wanted to be a cowboy so that I could hold back my tears and protect my family.

I used to smoke and drink, but then I quit both. I never learned how to drive, work the oil rigs, or ride a horse, but I did write songs about these things. I was not a cowboy in reality, but my heart always felt lonely enough to sing about it with conviction. When I'm scared, I stand tall and saunter around like my uncles. I make wry jokes out of the side of my mouth to protect myself. I have learned things that they don't tell you on the prairies, like that crying is a good thing, but I will always fall back on the kind toughness that I learned from my uncles whenever I feel completely alone.

Cowboy

I wanted you to think I was a cowboy,
So I told you where I am from.
But all I ever did was run from trucks
and I've never held a gun.

I wanted you to think I was strong,
So I showed you my restraint.
Far past when I lost control
I never stopped the game.

I wanted you to think I was a fighter,
So I showed you all of my teeth.
And I held them up like a monument
to the fall underneath

I wanted you to think I was a cowboy,
So I told you where I am from.
And I walked around like I didn't care
that I lost every one.

The Rest of My Chest

When I was young, they were way littler. In my early twenties, all I had to do really was bench press a bit of weight here and there, and they almost disappeared, I worked them down to muscly little apricots with nipples on them, easily hideable with a tight tank top and a t-shirt over top, then a long-sleeved shirt and a sweater and maybe a jacket. Then for a while I used Saran wrap, if you can believe that, in the good old days, back in the early nineties, Saran wrap but only for special occasions, of course, not for everyday, just for a fancy dinner or dress-up when you didn't want them messing up the line of your dress shirt like they do.

Then came the ACE bandages, but lucky for me those didn't last too too long before I started dating the dancer, and see, dancers mostly dance their breasts right off themselves, but also they have these flat elastic shirt things that the costume designers sew up for them to wear so they all look like androgynous willow trees, and once I got my hands on one of those elastic dancer shirt things, well, I never looked back.

Until my late thirties, at least, when all of a sudden they got

67

so much bigger, and then it was onwards to the double front compression shirt which sounds really heavy and constricting because it fucking is, right, and it is not made for guys like us, nothing really truly is made for us, it is mostly designed for cisgendered men and their man boobs and not really built to hold these ladies like mine, this pair that I went and grew myself somehow in the last six or seven years or so.

So. So. Nineteen years, I have been binding. Yes, thank you. I realize some of you are thinking, holy fuck, Saran wrap. That dude is old. And that is okay by me.

Where was I? Anyways, so all of a sudden a guy wakes up on the verge of forty-something years old and now not only do I have kind of big tits somehow but God being the joker that they are, I also have really nice big tits seriously sweet Jesus I wish it weren't so. Some days I look in the mirror and I think, whose are those? They are sweet but whoever left these here will hopefully come and take them away now because I need to put a shirt on and go outside.

That's the thing, right? I am totally fine with them when I am naked, well, mostly okay, unless you stare or take a side-view picture or touch them like this instead of like this or this, right, and so mostly I am okay with them naked, I suppose, unless you get all weird about them, in which case then I will definitely counter with feeling way weirder, but what I for sure all the time now definitely am not okay with is having these breasts on me unbound with my clothes on. Hard to describe, I guess, for those of you who feel actually attached in some way to all the parts of your body, or okay with every part of your body, because please, I know that it is not just trans people who feel like this about our bodies, but if you in fact feel perfectly okay with all the parts of the body you are travelling in right now then I say good on you, sincerely, I am glad for you, but it is not like that for me, you see, and I have tried and tried and tried for so long now and, well, I am pretty much certain it almost goes without saying at this point that chances are I am most likely not going to wake up one morning and say, okay, turns out it was all just a phase and only today I decided that I am totally fine having tits. In fact, look, look at my tits, I just love having them around.

This is probably not going to happen. And now, just lately, these three fingers have started tingling and going numb and the only thing that makes that tingling dead feeling go away is to take off the binder, and I am hoping it is not permanent nerve damage because I can't leave the house now at all with the ladies not tended to properly, just can't do it, can't really say why and don't need to anymore, so.

So I finally called my doctor. She referred me to a psychologist for a mental health assessment and diagnosis. I went to talk to that psychologist in her office downtown. I had never done anything like that before. That psychologist, she was way cooler than I thought she would be. I cried a lot more than I thought I was going to, and she asked a lot of questions about depression, general happiness, and my body. I tried to act not suicidal but not way too happy and well-adjusted, either. I am supposed to be here to get fixed, I know this already. So there has to be something wrong enough with me but not too wrong, not so wrong that I need different help from someone else that isn't her with something more pressing than I hate having these tits. Have to find that balance.

See, the thing is, I want top surgery, but I am not on hormones. Well, news flash, every single one of us is technically on hormones right now, but I am not taking any hormones, right, and this is not how it is supposed to go. I forget who wrote these rules, who decided the order of things, and why, and who decided hormones first then off come the tits, I don't know why there seems to be that rule, but I had to make a special case for myself that I was trans enough. In British Columbia, the province in Canada where I live, this surgery is covered by our health care system, provided you qualify. And by qualify, they mean be diagnosed. They, being the government. The government will pay for you to get fixed, but only if they decide you are broken in the right way. The other they being, in this case, the medical establishment. Before the bureaucrats can sign off on the form and send it to the surgeon, a psychologist and a psychiatrist must first decide if they believe me that I am who I say I am. In order to do this, I must fill out a long multiple-choice questionnaire, which the psychologist that my doctor referred me to will read through and assess, and then refer me to a psychiatrist for a proper diagnosis. Because someone who is trained in this stuff has to sign off that I do in fact have a bona fide gender identity disorder, but that someone cannot be me, because I am not qualified. And by gender identity disorder, they all mean that you want to be a man. Or a woman, as the case may be. It is not enough to just feel that you are not a woman or a man. You must want to be not the box that they have all previously put you in. There is no box to check for not wanting a box at all. No one knows how to fix that.

I had to be diagnosed with gender dysphoria, or gender identity disorder, and think about it, how would that feel to be told that just being yourself is a disorder, but if I don't say the right things and they don't say those words gender identity disorder, then I pay for everything out of pocket myself and I don't know about you but nine thousand dollars is a lot of money, and the question I keep on thinking but not asking that shrink is why can my cousin have two breast augmentations and get her lips filled with silicone, and no judgments here from me, because lord knows my poor cousin has received enough of it from our Catholic family, and she has been asked plenty of questions regarding who is paying for it all and why and what it might cost her in the long run, and ask her, just what exactly she feels it has all cost her in the end, but my question is, how come nobody makes her see a shrink first, yeah, but I don't ask that question because I need to catch more flies with honey or it's nine thousand bucks for me and I am already the wrong kind of trans guy because I don't want the hormones, I just want the breasts gone, well, not just gone, but the chest reconstruction too.

When I tell the psychologist that I use the "she" pronoun for work and in media interviews, she furrows her brow and writes faster on her pad of paper. When I tell her I have no intention of going on testosterone, she looks up at me, then down again and writes a bunch more stuff. I am starting to think about what I am not going to be able to do with that nine thousand dollars and how exactly am I gonna come up with it anyways. When the psychologist, who is actually pretty cool, asks me if I pack. As in a dick. As in, in my pants.

She asks me like she thinks I am going to say no. I can tell she doesn't think I am trans enough for this. Not to get it funded anyway.

Yes, I do, I say. I have been packing for over ten years easy, I tell her, maybe closer to fifteen. We used to make our own out of condoms and cheap hair gel and nylons. I told you. Fucking old school, man.

Well, then. She sits up straighter in her chair, starts writing some more.

I can't believe this, I say. Don't tell me this all comes down to whether or not I carry a dick in my pants.

She considers the implications of this for a minute.

I guess I am saying that, she admits.

I found this shocking at the time, but later, I had to admit it made a lot of sense. Just like the whole fucking world, and all those cocks, those cocks on people who want them on them anyways, and then I got to thinking about big cities all full of skyscrapers and hello, patriarchy, of course it comes down to my dick. Of course, having a dick in my pants and identifying on the masculine end of the spectrum makes all the difference. Especially when it comes to getting what I want.

The psychologist refers me to a psychiatrist for a formal diagnosis. Acquiring this diagnosis quickly became complicated for me, because there are very few psychiatrists in my province who the bureaucrats have certified to be allowed to make such an important decision about me, for me. On top of this, I have been writing about the gender binary and my place in it, or outside of it, for many years now, and one by one the psychiatrists that the bureaucrats had deemed qualified to decide if I was indeed transgendered enough to proceed with surgery were all forced to recuse themselves from making any decisions about me on ethical grounds, because they had read my work on gender in their how-to-be-nice-to-trans-people sensitivity workshop when they were going through the process of being trained to be certified to be allowed to make such decisions about people like me.

Make sense? I didn't think so. To sum it up, most of the psychiatrists who the government looked to so they could decide whether or not I was trans were unable to assess me because I had written about being trans, and they had read some of my work while learning about how to deal with trans people, and so were no longer objective enough to decide fairly if I was trans or not. This resulted in delays, and probably more paperwork. Conflict of whose interest, exactly? Interesting question.

Finally, the bureaucrats found a psychiatrist in a suburb who hadn't read any of my work on gender, and was thus naturally better equipped to understand and assess my gender for other professionals. Forms were filed. Letters were written. Decisions were made by those obviously more qualified than I am to understand myself.

I'm not saying it's a perfect system, but it's a health care system, and I am still grateful to reside in a country that possesses one.

As for this psychiatrist, I wanted to dislike him on principle but I could not seem to muster it up once we met in person. He had an Arthur Eames office chair, which I coveted very much, and we bonded over furniture (mid-century Danish teak modern) for a while before getting down to business. He proceeded to ask me a bunch more questions about my gender history, and my relationship with my father. He asked me how long I had been binding my breasts. I told him nineteen years.

His eyebrows shot up. Why so long? he asked, incredulous. Most of my patients come to me after about two weeks of that torture.

I don't like to rush into things, I told him.

He laughed so hard at that, a real genuine belly laugh too, and slapped his desk with a flat palm, so that I couldn't help but like him a little, despite myself. Couldn't help but wonder, though, just who else had been in my chair, because I knew tons of guys who had been binding for this long or even longer, guys who couldn't afford the cost or the time off, or who didn't have any health insurance at all, or who didn't jump through the right hoops or say the right things to the right suits. Turns out this guy mostly worked with adolescent trans kids.

Anyway, he wrote down stuff about my father issues, noted among other things that I was dapperly dressed and very punctual, which I appreciated, and sent me a copy of everything he wrote about me, which I also appreciated, and recommended me for gender reassignment surgery, without the usual pre-requisite hormone treatments.

My next question is for you. Am I trans enough now? Or, conversely, do you now feel that I no longer belong in the sisterhood? Did your feelings change at all for me over the course of this story? Do you find me more or less attractive? If so, why?

Please rate the strength of your feelings from one to five, one meaning you feel not very strongly about it all, to five meaning you have very strong feelings about me getting top surgery. Now, please fold up your answers and put them in your pocket. Please keep them to yourself, as I will try to do with my feelings about your breasts. Thank you so much for participating.

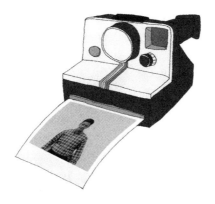

*I*n Fargo, North Dakota, I prepay $65 for gas. My tank will only take $53. I go back into the gas bar to get my change. "I guess I am used to Canadian gas prices," I explain. There is a random dude hanging around talking to the clerk. "You're from Canada?" he says. "We're, like, neighbours, aren't we?"

"Yeah," I say, "we are right on top of you."

He snorts. "Nobody is on top of us, you faggot. This is America."

"Technically," I say, backing out of the door, "*we* are on top of you. Geographically, not sexually."

"He's right," the female clerk says to the dude. "And go home now, Eddie, you are starting to get on my last nerve."

Prairie Gender

From far away, the ground cover on the prairies looks like a simple repetition of grass or wheat, but up close there are hundreds of plant species coexisting through extreme seasons and constant wind, working to survive. In the white, working-class, Protestant, anglophone prairie community that I grew up in, gender was just as complex as those plants. Of course, gender was dominated by the typical binary in terms of gender presentation and roles, but that was more of an official policy rather than an accurate description. In the messiness of life and sheer survival, there were constant contradictions. The women of my childhood were as tough as those low-lying thistles, and the only perceptible ways in which they were lesser than men was in the resources afforded to them and in how they were treated as inferior. The expectations placed on them were actually much higher than those placed on men. Most of these women survived in spite of their husbands, who often neglected, abused, and abandoned them and their children.

My grandmother grew up in Saskatchewan. Her father owned the John Deere dealership in the small town where they lived, and she worked there selling farm equipment when she was a teenager. My grandmother would pull me onto her knee and tell me stories about Saskatchewan winters and driving tractors around the store lot. She told me that her father was lax with her about things like that because she had shown interest in running his business. When it came time to marry, she found a young Irish preacher with bright blue eyes and jet black hair. He told her stories about wanting to settle down in a small town in Alberta, about starting a family and spreading God's word. After their sixth child was born, however, my grandfather's passions wavered from both Christ and his family, and he ran off with an elementary school teacher from the town. I have never heard anything about what that did to my grandmother, other than that she raised her six children alone from then on. A man abandoning his children at that time was not unusual, while a woman who did the same thing would be considered monstrous. Like a lot of single mothers, my grandmother ended up doing all of the stereotypical work of both men and women, but with very little appreciation. She moved the family to Calgary, got a job at a bank, and continued to care for her children by herself. After her children were grown, she retired to a small house in the northeast of Calgary, where she mowed her own lawn and watched sports on the television.

My mother was considered a tomboy in school because she was athletic and could run faster than anyone else. As a teenager, she wore cowboy boots, and smoked and drank along with the boys. She was famous for her temper and has stories about throwing rocking chairs at her brothers during arguments. She worked on a farm during high school to pay her room and board, delivering calves and driving tractors. As an adult, my mother withstood seventeen years of living with my abusive father when she thought she had no other choice. After my parents divorced, she followed my grandmother's example and put herself through college while raising her four children. She got an office job after she graduated.

Many of my aunts stayed at home while my uncles were away working on the oil rigs for months at a time. The women checked their own oil in their trucks and fed their own horses while doing chores and raising children. Their husbands would work for months at a time in northern Alberta or in Saskatchewan, and when my uncles did come home they would have money burning a hole in their pockets, so they would often go out partying and gambling. The day-to-day business of running a household, including what would be thought of as men's work, fell to my aunts by default.

When I was a child, I didn't know that I would ever identify as a man. I didn't do that until I saw it as an option, and I had to leave the prairies in order to do so. But I also couldn't imagine growing up to be a woman. My father would often say to me and my sister, "You're going to end up barefoot and pregnant before you know it!" He would say this with a sardonic grin. After my mother left him, I helped her raise my two younger brothers. Even as a child, I felt trapped and exhausted by housework and childcare. I knew that I was supposed to be a girl, but I never let my mind rest for long on what seemed like an unwanted yet impending fate. I used my imagination to survive, and I decided that I could be any manner of things, anything but a woman raising children alone in Alberta. How exactly I was going to evade being trapped was not something I could yet fathom.

Once I identified as a man, I found it as impossible to play the stereotypical male role as it was to play the female one. This was not only because society and individual people were constantly telling me that I wasn't a "real" man because of the body I inhabited, but also because sexism made me just as uncomfortable when I was on the side with more power. There was a lot of pressure from the queer community, and from outside of it, to earn my identity as a man by acting like one. To cross from one side of the binary to the other, I was expected to prove that I was, in fact, male. So for a time, I shied away from femininity because I thought it would not help my cause. At the same time, I felt hesitant to defend my place in the binary because it inevitably led to putting women down. I knew through experience that men were not stronger or better than women, and that masculinity was not better than femininity. I knew that men did not all behave one way and women another. But that didn't make things any easier.

Creating a false narrative about my own gender would be turning my back on that history. When I was a man, I wasn't comfortable subscribing to the division of certain activities like changing oil on a car or wearing makeup. I can't say that I learned to be tough only from my cowboy, oil-rig-working, truck-driving uncles. It was the women who were expected to hold everything together, and that they did. As a transgender person, I don't have the acceptance of most of my family. I've crossed a line that they see as uncrossable. However, when I'm standing up for myself, or laying low in order to survive as a trans person, I use skills that the women in my family taught me. I am not a woman, but I am fighting against the same elements for survival. I am proud to stand next to the women in my family as a survivor. I feel like it's a sentiment that they would understand. We are like two different kinds of plants bending next to each other in the prairie wind.

Tender Failure Theme Song

Bm
I will be your

failure.

G
I will be your

failure.

Gender Identity Interview for Adults (FtM)

For each statement, circle whether this has been true for you Always, Often, Sometimes, Rarely, or Never. Please use the space provided to add any comments should you wish.

1. In the past 12 months, have you felt satisfied being a woman?

    ☐ Always   ☐ Often   ☐ Sometimes   ☐ Rarely   ☐ Never

2. In the past 12 months, have you felt uncertain about your gender, that is, feeling somewhere in between a woman and a man?

    ☐ Always   ☐ Often   ☐ Sometimes   ☐ Rarely   ☐ Never

3. In the past 12 months, have you felt pressured by others to be a man, although you don't really feel like one?

    ☐ Always   ☐ Often   ☐ Sometimes   ☐ Rarely   ☐ Never

4. In the past 12 months, have you, unlike most women, felt that you have to work at being a woman?

    ☐ Always   ☐ Often   ☐ Sometimes   ☐ Rarely   ☐ Never

5. In the past 12 months, have you felt that you were not a real woman?

    ☐ Always   ☐ Often   ☐ Sometimes   ☐ Rarely   ☐ Never

6. In the past 12 months, have you felt, given who you really are (e.g., what you like to do, how you act with other people), that it would be better for you to live as a man rather than as a woman?

    ☐ Always   ☐ Often   ☐ Sometimes   ☐ Rarely   ☐ Never

7. In the past 12 months, have you had dreams?

☐ Yes   ☐ No

If NO, skip to question 8

If YES, Have you been in your dreams?

☐ Yes   ☐ No

If YES, In the past 12 months, have you had dreams in which you were a man?

☐ Always   ☐ Often   ☐ Sometimes   ☐ Rarely   ☐ Never

8. In the past 12 months, have you felt unhappy about being a woman?

☐ Always   ☐ Often   ☐ Sometimes   ☐ Rarely   ☐ Never

9. In the past 12 months, have you felt uncertain about yourself, at times feeling more like a man and at times feeling more like a woman?

☐ Always   ☐ Often   ☐ Sometimes   ☐ Rarely   ☐ Never

10. In the past 12 months, have you felt more like a man than a woman?

☐ Always   ☐ Often   ☐ Sometimes   ☐ Rarely   ☐ Never

11. In the past 12 months, have you felt that you did not have anything in common with either men or women?

☐ Always   ☐ Often   ☐ Sometimes   ☐ Rarely   ☐ Never

12. In the past 12 months, have you been bothered by seeing yourself identified as female or having to check the box "F" for female in official terms?

☐ Always   ☐ Often   ☐ Sometimes   ☐ Rarely   ☐ Never

13. In the past 12 months, have you felt comfortable when using women's restrooms in public places?

☐ Always   ☐ Often   ☐ Sometimes   ☐ Rarely   ☐ Never

14. In the past 12 months, have strangers treated you as a man?

☐ Always   ☐ Often   ☐ Sometimes   ☐ Rarely   ☐ Never

15. In the past 12 months, at home have people you know, such as friends or relatives, treated you as a man?

☐ Always   ☐ Often   ☐ Sometimes   ☐ Rarely   ☐ Never

16. In the past 12 months, have you had the wish or desire to be a man?

☐ Always   ☐ Often   ☐ Sometimes   ☐ Rarely   ☐ Never

17. In the past 12 months, at home, have you dressed and acted like a man?

☐ Always   ☐ Often   ☐ Sometimes   ☐ Rarely   ☐ Never

Man Failure, Part 1

Micah, a friend of mine, was the supervisor at the gas station I worked at during and after high school. One afternoon I walked in with my too-big blue uniform shirt untucked over my black cargo pants, and he already looked amused. Usually I had to crack a joke or trip over something to see that glow in his eyes.

"A lady came in today," he said.

"Yeah?" I grunted.

"She said that she came in yesterday and got her oil checked. She needed a quart of oil and we put one in."

I stayed silent and shifted my weight.

"Anyways, she was pretty pissed off. Said she was served by a young man with a shaved head. Said he put a quart of oil in, but left the cap off her oil tank. Her whole engine was covered in the stuff by the time she got home."

I kept my hands close to my sides, trying to not run them through my quarter-inch long hair. "That sucks," I said, not owning up to my mistake.

"Well, the manager gave her a coupon to have her engine

shampooed. Pretty expensive stuff. She can't figure out which member of the staff it was, though. We don't have any boys working here that match that description." He struggled to finish without laughing, and our eyes met in acknowledgment. We both knew that I was the boy who messed up that engine, but the manager would have been too embarrassed to acknowledge it or point it out. I don't know if I've ever been as grateful for my legal status as female as at that moment, or for the stigma of pointing out that I was being mistaken for a male.

Micah didn't rat me out to the manager. I kept my job and went on to make a lot of other mistakes, servicing cars and sometimes being asked if I was old enough to work there when the legal working age in Alberta at the time was fourteen. I was sometimes seen as a boy before I ever felt like I was allowed to say I was one. People just thought I was, and I wouldn't argue to save time. Or, maybe I liked it as long as it didn't get too awkward. I was sure I'd find answers when I had the chance to meet more gay people. I couldn't wait to turn eighteen so I could go to gay and lesbian bars. Maybe I might discover a place where I fit in.

I had found out about the lesbian bar in Calgary from a queer singer-songwriter I'd met at open mic night at a café downtown, and I had scrawled down the information on the back of a handbill, which I saved for when I was old enough to use it. At the end of January, two weeks after turning eighteen, I stood in the line outside of Rooks breathing into my scarf to keep warm and clutching my plastic learner's license in my hand, hidden from the cold in the sleeve of my coat. I brought Micah and my gay friend Steve because I was scared of going alone. The bouncer eyed my ID a bit longer than the others', but then she just shrugged and let us in. Inside, the heat of the place hit us and my glasses immediately fogged up. When I wiped them off and put them back on, I saw that it was a well-lit, wood-panelled pub. There were booths along the walls, and half of them were full of women seated or standing in front of them. There were women standing, and some perched on stools along the bar too. Some of them were wearing dresses and some were wearing men's clothes like me. My heart jumped a bit. We went to the bar, ordered a pitcher of Canadian with three glasses, and settled down in a free booth. "So what do we do now?" asked Micah.

"I don't know," I said. I hadn't really thought about how I was supposed to meet people here, and no one had looked at us since we came in besides the bouncer and the bartender. It slowly dawned on me that I had no plan whatsoever. I had pictured the lesbians at the bar recognizing me for what I was and welcoming us to hang out with them at one of the tables. This was clearly not the way things were done around there, so I settled in and waited.

After twenty minutes of staring at Micah and Steve in silence, I noticed a sign over a descending staircase that read, "Rooks Club." Our beers were half gone, so I poured the rest of the pitcher to top up our glasses. "Hey, dudes. Let's go downstairs."

Steve shrugged so we all stood up and shuffled down the staircase. A thumping beat became more pronounced as we descended. At the bottom of the stairs, there was a door that led into a dark room at the end of a brightly lit hall. As we stepped inside, all of the balled-up lint on our winter sweaters started to glow. Micah smiled when he realized it was due to the black light, and his teeth lit up blue. The music was overpowering techno; with a robotic voice, the Daft Punk song played: "Around the world, around the world. Around the world." There were only two people there besides us, a woman with glowing plastic eyebrow rings, who was DJing, and her friend with bright pink hair who was leaning across the table shouting in her ear. "I'm not so sure about this room either," I yelled at Micah.

He leaned over to Steve and asked, "Do you want to go to the washroom together?"

Steve nodded. That's when I realized that they were the only men in the bar.

"I'm going outside to smoke. It's too hot in here," I said to them as they headed to the other side of the dark room where a washroom sign was lit up.

I walked up the stairs feeling defeated, not sure that I was ever going to meet new lesbians. I had been having a hard time since my break-up with my first girlfriend the summer after high school. I had found her through what felt like luck, but ever since it seemed like my luck had run out. I zipped up my coat and pushed open the back door to the alley. I fished a cigarette out of my pocket and lit it, exhaling upwards toward the night sky. Suddenly a woman with dyed purple hair came out of the bar. She leaned on the wall near me, and asked, "What's your name? I think I saw you sing at one of those bars downtown."

"Rae," I said. "I've been playing a bunch of open stages."

Then she asked, without telling me her name, "Do you know those guys who were in the bar tonight?"

"Yeah," I said. "That's Micah and Steve. They're my best friends."

"I'm a separatist, and I don't appreciate men being here," she said coolly.

I squinted quizzically at her. She seemed to be from Alberta, not Québec, Canada's francophone province whose population often wants to separate from the rest of the country. I had never met a Québecois separatist before, but I remembered the referendum when I was younger. The context didn't really make a lot of sense to me. Luckily for me, she continued before I asked her any questions.

"You know … like a separatist from men? I have no use for men in my life and anyone who does isn't welcome here. It's not feminist."

Was that why a lot of the women at Rooks had been so cold to me and my friends? Because they didn't like men? I liked Micah and Steve a lot, and I couldn't really see the difference between us or how their being men would be a bad thing, even if I was a lesbian. I started to feel a lot colder than it was outside. "I gotta go," I said to her, and stomped out my cigarette butt in the snow. I pulled the door open and found Micah and Steve inside, backed into one of the corners by the pool tables, chatting uneasily. They must have gone back upstairs while I was smoking. Quietly, Steve said to me, "I don't think that Micah and I are very welcome here. I'm gay, but not the right kind of gay, I think."

"I know," I said. "I don't really want to hang out anywhere where we aren't all welcome. Let's get out of here."

Micah drove us back to the suburbs in his old car, and we played pool in the pub a few blocks from where we lived. I felt more at home there than I had at Rooks. We went there all the time. It was pretty much like every other night we had spent together since we had become friends: staving off the boredom with jokes, and drinking until our jokes became funnier. Steve and I talked about how we were unsure if either of us would ever find someone to date again. The gay bars he had gone to had not been much friendlier. "I don't think they would let you in to some of them," he said.

I knew that being friends with Micah and Steve was more important than getting a thousand phone numbers on little pieces of paper at Rooks. I had failed at that lesbian bar by bringing men with me, but I felt that my friends knew me as well as I could expect anyone to. I was glad that we had all ended up together in the end.

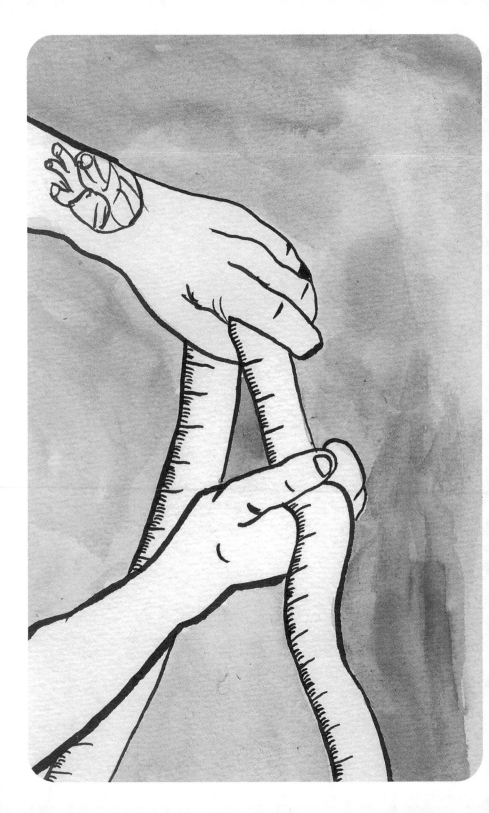

Thirteen Inches, Uncut

I was so nervous, the secretary at the reception desk looked at me with softening eyes and told me everything was going to be okay. I had barely spoken to her, but it was just that obvious, I guess.

First of all, it didn't feel like there was any possible way this could really be happening. Nineteen years of binding my breasts, even more years trying not to hate them, a psychologist's appointment, a psychiatrist's appointment, a psychological assessment, two doctor's appointments, several letters back and forth between doctors and shrinks and bureaucrats, phone calls, more phone calls, twenty months since I had actually cranked the whole machine into gear, and here I was. Meeting the surgeon. He was fourteen minutes late. But who was counting?

He was handsome and tanned in January, and his assistant was tall, blonde, and wearing grey leather stiletto boots. Looked pretty much like what I thought a cosmetic surgeon and his assistant would look like, not that I had ever spent much time wondering. I have to fill out forms, of course, no I don't smoke or have hemophilia, and no, my religion does not forbid me to have a blood transfusion. The letterhead on the forms is for a cosmetic surgery clinic. I am reminded that most people think that is what this is. Elective. Cosmetic. Unnecessary. My period is due today. My tits are at their biggest, and most tender. I can feel the binder pinching under my arms where it does.

Turns out the doctor and I both studied music at a small community college together in the late eighties. I do not remember him, and he would not recognize me. I ask him if he studied jazz piano just in case this whole cosmetic surgeon thing didn't work out for him, you know, so he had something to fall back on. I make jokes like that sometimes when I am nervous.

He asks me a lot of questions. Why am I not on testosterone? Do I intend to go on testosterone in the future? What do I want my chest to look like when he is done? Do I care more about what my chest looks like, or whether or not I will be able to feel my nipples afterwards? I tell him a little of both. This surprises him. He tells me it is mostly only women who care about nipple sensation after surgery, and that most trans men only care that they have a masculine appearing chest after. He looks at his assistant, is she getting all of this down? And she nods back just a little, yes, she is.

Throughout this entire bureaucratic maze, I have wanted to not like the doctors, the psychiatrist, the surgeon. The gatekeepers. I have been waiting for one of them to be callous, or say something phobic or use the wrong pronoun, or write the wrong thing down on the wrong form. But everyone has been so ... nice. Even though I still care about whether or not I can feel my nipples afterwards. I never quite feel like they truly understand me, but that doesn't seem to get in the way of them completing the task at hand.

I have to strip my upper body and put on a blue gown. The surgeon measures my chest extensively. I haven't worn a typical woman's bra in my entire life, and I don't mean there is any such thing as a typical woman, let me be clear, what I mean is a bra-type article of clothing typically worn by a woman, anyway, I have never owned or worn one, ever since I was nineteen or so and they finally appeared on the scene uninvited, I have always tried to mash them down, disappear them, never lift and separate, so I actually have no idea how big they really are. Turns out I have a forty-two-inch chest, a number that seems surreal to me, nearly impossible. I explain to the surgeon that they didn't used to be this big, just since I hit my forties, my body is changing, and if he performed double hipectomies I would be signing up for that, too. He is calling out measurements and observations to his assistant. My breast tissue is dense and firm, he states. She scribbles on her notepad. My nipples are big and will have to be removed completely from my body and resized and grafted back onto me. He remarks that my breasts exhibit very little ptosis, which is a medical term for sagging. This makes me feel oddly proud, considering I am here to have them removed. Kind of like waxing up your car so you can take it to the wrecker, or petting a puppy before you leave it out in the cold. Which, for the record, I would never do. I love puppies. But even talking aloud about it all felt kind of like that for me, like I was closing a door on a room I really loved, only because it was the one way I knew to keep going.

He pulls out a blue Sharpie and makes several marks on my chest, then stands back and surveys them. Like you would if you were trying to hang a picture level on a wall. Then he takes a camera out, snaps several pictures of me from the neck down, and then puts it away.

He explains to me that I will need a double incision/bi-lateral mastectomy, and that my nipples will be rendered insensate. He delivers this news deadpan, like he's has had a lot of practice saying these words without any affectation or emotion whatsoever. Insensate. I looked it up after, later, when I got home. It has two meanings: 1: lacking physical sensation. And 2: lacking sympathy or compassion, unfeeling.

The surgeon narrows his eyes at my copious chest hair. "You have never taken testosterone?" he asks me again. I shake my head, no. "Well, there is something going on for you here, then," he tells me.

"Positive thinking," I tell him, and he smiles, like this can't be true, even though I am pretty sure it is.

He measures my nipples from tip to tip, lets out a low whistle. "Wow," he says, sounding impressed. "Thirteen inches." His assistant raises her head, looks over at us, writes it down. I have no idea what this means, whether this number is impressive because it is so small, or so big.

"Yep," I state. "That's right. Thirteen inches, uncut." We all crack up. My nipples are standing on their tiptoes now, maybe from the cool air in the examination room, maybe from brushing up against the measuring tape, maybe from fear. Hard to say.

I did and still do wonder why he wasn't using the metric system of measurement. Thirty-three point zero two centimeters sounds way more accurate somehow, even though the metric system is decidedly less sexy. Maybe that is why the United States stubbornly holds on to the standard system of measurement. Its undeniable erotic potential. Thirteen inches seems impressive, especially when it is a body part of any sort. And ninety miles an hour sounds so much hotter and faster than one hundred and forty-four point eight four kilometers ever could.

The next morning, I looked long at myself in the mirror. Tried to imagine my new chest. Touched my exquisitely sensitive nipples. Imagined them small, and dull to touch, and stitched back on. I have done this a million times before. But this time there were two blue marks, in the soft crease there, dead centre below my nipples. I had scrubbed and scrubbed at them in the shower, but they wouldn't come off, they had hardly even faded. The ink the surgeon had used had been very, very permanent.

Man Failure, Part 2

When I was nineteen, I moved to Vancouver because it felt a lot more open there compared to the prairies, except, of course, for the landscape. It wasn't as hard to find queer people to hang out with, and I even found a girlfriend after a while. I started feeling more optimistic about being part of an accepting community.

One night I was out drinking at the downtown Legion on East Pender with my new girlfriend Cora. It was crowded and there weren't a lot of places to sit. We ended up next to some people, two girls and a guy, who looked familiar but whom neither of us had met before. I couldn't make out their names as they shouted them over the Friday night din. Later on, I found myself debating loudly with one of the girls, whose name turned out to be Kelly, about something that felt urgent at the time in my drunken state. Kelly nodded toward the other girl and said, "Jeremiah thinks the same thing. He's always going on about it, so don't try to convince me. I made up my mind a long time ago."

I paused. "Her name is Jeremiah?"

"*His* name is Jeremiah," she responded tersely. I pushed forward, wanting to understand, and looked closely at Jeremiah again. He had a boyish face and smallish tattooed arms, and I noticed that his chest was flat. But his voice was high when he spoke, and earlier I had heard him squeal with laughter.

"Jeremiah is a guy?" I asked, with confusion in my voice.

"Yes. He's trans," she said, flustered.

What does that mean? I thought to myself. I think Kelly saw the look on my face, realized I didn't know what it meant, and took pity on me.

"He was assigned female at birth, but has chosen to identify as a man. So he wants to be called 'he' and treated like a guy."

"You mean like a sex change?" I asked.

"Sort of, but you're not supposed to call it that," she said.

I curled inward a bit. I felt like I'd said a lot of things wrong without meaning to. I leaned over to Cora and said, "You see that person, Jeremiah? He's trans and he wants to be treated like a guy." She looked like she couldn't hear me, but I knew she could.

I continued my conversation with Kelly, stumbling on *he*s where I would have moments before used *she*s. It turned out that the other guy with them, Anton, was also trans but was taking testosterone he'd bought on the black market, which had helped him to grow a beard and big muscles. I felt mesmerized as I studied his hairy face and the flat chests on both him and Jeremiah. Suddenly choice came crashing in like a great wave. It was right in front of me, embodied by my new friends.

The next morning, I woke up next to Cora in my bedroom, hung over. My head was pounding, but there was something more important than a headache inside it. I rolled away from her and asked, "I wonder how Jeremiah gets his chest so flat?"

There was a long pause and I wondered if she was still asleep.

"Why would you want to know that?" she finally asked.

"I don't know. I think it would be cool if I could do it too. I mean, I didn't know that I could until I saw it," I replied.

"That would be pretty weird," she said coolly. "I mean, it would be kind of disgusting if we made out and you were like that. Besides, you're not a boy, are you?"

"I don't know," I mumbled.

Cora and I broke up soon after that conversation. I did find out how I could flatten my chest from Jeremiah the next time we hung out. I also told him that I wanted to be treated like a guy and referred to as "he" too. It felt so great when we parted and he said to me, "See you later, man."

I went to a drugstore and bought an ACE bandage like he told me, binding my chest flat by wrapping it around me. It would ride up while I was at work washing dishes in a kitchen, causing me to take numerous adjustment breaks, but it made me feel lighter. My roommate caught me putting it on in our bathroom and told me that she would call me "he" if I wanted, but that she would never see me as a man.

I told a few people at work that I was friends with that I wanted them to refer to me as "he," but one of the servers kept referring to me as "she." After I'd cleaned out the dish pit one night, we all went to the bar, where she called me a lady and used "she" a couple more times. At the end of the night outside the bar, when we were all drunk, I asked her, "Why can't you call me 'he'?" I was shaking with anger.

"Well, you have hips," she said. "I guess I just see you as a girl because of it."

Within a week of changing my pronoun of choice to "he," I realized what an uphill battle it was going to be, but I didn't want to stop flattening my chest and being a guy. It felt a lot better than how I had been before, even if I had to convince a lot of people that I was a man. I decided to stay true to my choice. If I showed that I really meant it, everyone would have to refer to me as "he" eventually, I thought.

Ten years later, I was visiting Vancouver to facilitate some workshops for a feminist music camp. I didn't identify as a woman, but the life I live on the outside of my body was far from being steeped in male privilege. I had been both a girl and a musician as a teenager, so I wanted to help build the confidence of the girls in the workshop. I had seen so few women in the music industry, and I wanted to do everything I could to make sure that there were more. I was standing outside that same Legion on East Pender with a group of queer people I knew. I had long since quit smoking and drinking, but I was always willing to hang out with old friends at bars. There was a trans guy named Mark standing with us, and he asked me what I was doing in town. I'd known him since he was a teenager in Nelson, because he had come to one of my shows there and later I'd mailed him a copy of a book that Ivan had written with the collective Taste This, entitled *Boys Like Her*. I wanted to help him wait out the last couple years of his time as a queer kid in a small town with some company, even if they were words in a book.

"I'm doing workshops at the feminist music camp," I told him. "It's going to be awesome!"

"Oh," he replied. "I'm volunteering there too, but it's going to be weird being the only guy there."

My blood went cold. I was used to being misgendered by strangers, but I'd always gone by "he" as long as this guy had known me.

"Yeah, except me, right?" I said, hoping he'd correct himself.

"Yeah, I know, but I'm on hormones, so they just think I'm a man and you're not. They think you're a girl. It's a lot harder for me to be in women's spaces."

I opened my mouth to respond, but then shut it. I didn't know where to begin to express how invisible I felt.

• • •

If being a man is something that required a person to tick off a bunch of boxes, not many people would make it through. Many cisgendered men (people assigned male at birth who are comfortable with that assignment) are unable to grow a beard, have a high voice, or have larger chests and hips. If the gender binary was enforced based only on body characteristics, very few people would be read as a man or a woman. Being subject to criticism on how I had failed to have enough body characteristics to be read as male by most people changed my mind about the system of gender designation itself. I decided that breaking apart people's bodies to classify them as a specific gender is wrong because it hurt me so many times when people did it to me. Now I resist the urge within myself to use people's bodies to drop them into easily categorized boxes. It's not something I do perfectly, but it's a way of thinking that makes me feel like I am making space in the world for gender variance. I hope in the future that asking to be regarded as any gender will be enough, even if I know it's probably a distant future.

My failure to be accepted as a man by many people was rooted mainly in my failure to strive toward the physical traits stereotypically associated with masculinity as if they were the highest points on a hill. I was not willing to lose other parts of myself to attain all of the body characteristics that would be required to be read as male in public. My body is something that I have grown not to hate just because it isn't stereotypically male. I don't think there is a way to define a male body, and I no longer believe in the system of classification that never fit me.

Top Surgery

Somewhere between lying in bed convinced that I won't sleep at all, and waking up just before the alarm goes off, all the nervous and the worry slips away, leaving me in a strange state of calm and readiness. I take a deep breath. Surgery day.

I shower and carefully wash my breasts and chest and underarms with the antiseptic cleanser, just as instructed in the handout from the surgeon's office. The handout was a strange hybrid of materials, some generic information culled together for plastic surgery patients of all varieties, some that seemed to address women who were having breast reductions or augmentations, and some specifically directed towards trans-masculine people having "top surgery," written for some reason in quotations. I always question the use of quotations around things that are not actually quotes. Did the author mean for us to read the words with one eyebrow raised, as in "top surgery, question mark, question mark?" What are we being asked to double check? Is this an invitation to question the honesty of the speaker, or the subject matter? Is this an alias? Who is suspect here, and why? Quotation marks around words that are not actually quotes are the literary equivalent of being told to report all suspicious behaviour and not to leave your bag unattended and not to accept any packages from strangers. The orange alert of sentence structure.

I am on my way to having my "top surgery." Zena, my partner, and I go about our morning rituals quietly and sweetly, touching each other gently by the sink, smiling in the mirror together. I am not permitted to eat or drink anything, so my morning ritual is short. I am dressed early and sit on the couch and watch the blue sky burn through the last of the morning mist, trying not to make her feel rushed out the door. She takes my ID and health care card and tucks them into her purse, and places my paperwork and post-operative compression vest on the counter by the door so we don't forget them. As if we could forget anything on this morning, having prepared and thought about it all for months as we both have.

We talk softly a little in the cab, and arrive early on purpose. The clinic is clean and quiet, the front desk empty, and I can smell coffee brewing from somewhere behind the door that leads into the hallway on the other side of the newly styled waiting room. This is no public hospital or clinic, the evidence of that is everywhere. This is a private surgical clinic, American-style, right here in the West End of Vancouver. We crack jokes that we don't really mean about maybe re-thinking this whole two-tiered medical system after all, and survey the view of Davie Street and the skyscrapers lined up along the shores of English Bay. The receptionist returns to her desk and greets us efficiently. The phone rings and she answers it, and I hear her subdued tone as she explains to the person on the other end, obviously another staff member of some sort, that this morning there is an ankle, an amputated toe, and a double mastectomy on the roster. The staff start to trickle in, a handsome male nurse with still-wet-from-the-shower brown curls, a kind-eyed man who will turn out to be my anesthesiologist.

We are ushered into a small room. I strip and place my clothes into a large plastic bag that says "PATIENT'S BELONGINGS" on it, and put on the blue gown and thin robe, booties, and hair net that have been laid out for me. The nurse comes in and checks my blood pressure and heart rate. He tells me I show absolutely no physical signs of being nervous, and he is right. Zena seems more restless than I do. She has little purple bags showing under her worried eyes. I calmly swallow some pills, an anti-nausea one and some Tylenol, I think it was. He places a plastic band around my wrist.

The anesthesiologist comes in and explains the procedure to me. I can hear the nurse outside the door now, talking about weekend barbecues and hockey and the weather. This is a normal day at work for them. This life-changing day for me, this before-and-forever-after day, is another Monday morning for everybody else.

The surgeon has arrived and comes into the room. He calls me by my legal birthname, and I correct him. This is not really his fault. I have never changed my name legally, so that is what it says on my file, and it has been five months since the one and only time we ever met in person. He asks me to pull down my robe and gown and tie them around my waist. He whips out a Sharpie and marks my breasts and chest, sketching arcs and making marks like a painter or a carpenter or a sculptor. He stands back, holds up a thumb, closes one eye, adjusts the marks. The entire process takes only a few minutes, and I am shocked at how arbitrary and casual it all seems. I think about the saying my dad used to repeat over and over when we were building things or doing stuff in the shop together: "Measure twice, cut once." I think this over and over but don't say it. It also seems outrageous to me that I am being marked up with a Sharpie, like a Tupperware container or a cardboard moving box. Aren't there surgical-grade felt pens for this kind of thing? Steripen? Surgimark? No. Medium point plain black Sharpie, it is.

(As I write these words right now, it is exactly one week later, Monday morning, June 10, 8:19 a.m. To the minute, seven days have passed since I hugged my wife and walked down the hallway and into the operating room. There is still black ink on my chest, a fading line of it trailing down to a blurred streak under the clear adhesive bandage that is covering the bandages that hide my new chest from me. The black ink has turned dark purple, like a bleeding and faded tattoo on your uncle's freckled forearm. I haven't been able to wash it off because I am not allowed to shower or bathe until the drains come out.)

The anesthesiologist is now wearing a mask and gown, but I recognize his eyes. One of the nurses has a Scottish accent. The other nurse, not the Scottish one, calls me "she" as she reads out some information to the doctor, then pauses and corrects herself. I pretend not to notice. I climb up onto the operating table. I had somehow imagined being wheeled in already on a gurney, but that is not how it is. The nurses place surgical stockings on my legs and a thin blanket on the lower half of my body. I feel a tiny prick on the top of my left hand, and the anesthesiologist asks me to tell him about the books I write. "Well," I told him, "I have seven collections of short stories, one novel, and my wife and I edited an anthology, mostly non-fiction, about butch and femme … "

Then I heard my name being called and a different woman's voice, in a thick Eastern European accent, telling me it is all over, that I had done really well. There is a clock on the wall on the other side of the paper curtain half-drawn around my hospital bed, but I cannot make my eyes focus enough to read what time it is. I am unbelievably cold, my teeth chattering, and thirstier than I ever remember feeling. I have to pee, and my stomach is rumbling empty. I force my eyes to focus slowly on the clock again. I look down. Tears of relief flood my eyes and run down my cheeks. Nearly four hours have somehow disappeared. So have my breasts.

My Body Is a Spaceship

Growing up in the nudity-free zone that was Pentecostal shame meant that my first awareness of my own body was in draping flower patterns over it to cover myself. The no-shirts-off-for-girls rule was in full effect as far back as I can remember. I could have been the invisible man underneath my clothes for all I knew, and I never spent a lot of time reflecting on my body in its resting state. It was in movement that I could feel myself in my body. Biking, rollerblading, running, climbing trees, and building forts were what my body felt good for. It was a digging machine, a stick swinger, a lemur, and, when I was going too fast down a hill to hear anything but the hum of my skateboard's wheels, it was a spaceship in search of aliens on a distant planet.

I needed all the space armour I could get when I hit puberty. I didn't want to give too much thought to how the outside of me was changing, or the fact that I felt better huddled inside my body like it contained a secret place that I could control. People started to tell me that I was becoming a woman, but I knew that that was just on the outside; inside, I was going to stay the same: ambivalent to the confusing expectations that surrounded me.

By the time I was twelve, things in my family had become very unstable. My father had been institutionalized after a breakdown, and I started to use my detached state to shelter myself from that too. I felt like I didn't have any control over anything, so I decided to try to control the one thing I could: I stopped eating. I liked the euphoric state that I would get into when I threw out my lunch and ran on adrenaline for the rest of the day. After a while I started to see, by weighing myself, that I was having an effect on my body. That only made my resolve grow. It was a way of saying "I don't want to be here" without using words. Fat became my enemy. Not because I wanted to look like the typical 1990s model, but because it was something about my changing body that I could control, and I had come to hate my body. I thought there was something wrong with it. I wanted to get as far away from what I was as I could. At that point I didn't know that I had any choice in gender, so I never made the connection that I was evading the inevitable role of being assigned female by trying to keep my body from becoming one, and not giving it the fuel it needed to develop.

I made the choice to try to stop starving myself after I moved out on my own when I was eighteen. Being queer from a Pentecostal family meant that I didn't have much of a safety net, and so I resolved to try to change unsustainable patterns of behaviour before they put me in a position as vulnerable as the one I had just fled. I didn't want my family to have control over me ever again, and I knew that starving myself might put me in the hospital or, worse, back in their care. Slowly I managed to start eating again, and I even banned weighing myself altogether. In time, I did gain weight, although I still had no way of judging the appearance of my own body. There has always been a dysphoria between how I think I look and how I am told I look. I never did entirely lose the compulsion to stop eating, but now it visits periodically instead of ruling over my entire routine.

When I was twenty and found out that gender was an option, I decided to identify as a man. The narrative seemed to fit me. The recurring discomfort that I had experienced made a lot more sense if I had been a man trapped in a woman's body. I thought that my body had been the problem all along, but then the urges to change it returned. Instead of looking at the varied bodies of the men around me, I leaned toward the stereotypical body that I thought a man was supposed to have. If only I could change my body to make it look more like what men were supposed to look like: wider shoulders, flat chest, narrower hips, bigger muscles, hairier face. No wonder I had been so uncomfortable without all of that.

A lot of my trans male friends had started taking testosterone and began exhibiting one or more of these characteristics, becoming read more and more often as male in public. I was anxious to join them even though it was a long process of jumping through bureaucratic hoops and paying for surgeries. But there was a problem: my voice. The testosterone would not only make it lower, but would potentially alter how much control I had over it. My music career had taken off when I turned twenty. I was getting more positive reinforcement about my voice than I had ever gotten about anything else. It made singing too hard to let go of or gamble with. So I chose not to take hormones, though this decision was not an easy one at all.

During this time, I imagined myself travelling in a better, more improved spaceship, one that would protect me from those who didn't understand what being transgender meant, and from the long conversations I had to have in order to explain it. I wanted a body that would protect me from those who still referred to me as "she" even after such explanations. I longed to correct the things that made people perceive me as a woman, and to be able to lay low inside of myself.

I focused on the qualities of my body that kept me from appearing to be a man. I was hard on my hips. I thought they were too wide to be a boy's. I hated that my chest stuck out, but I was really tired of binding with an ACE bandage. No matter how I wrapped it around myself, it always managed to slouch down lower after a short period of time, often achieving the counterproductive function of actually pushing my chest up from below and making it look bigger than it was. My voice, the main asset of my music career, was the subject of so much self-hatred. It allowed me to sing certain notes and even yodel, but at the same time it was high-pitched and gave me away immediately if I was being read as a man at all in a situation. But there was no having it two ways. I could take hormones or I could sing the way I did. I couldn't have both.

When I was twenty-one, I had the great luck of discovering amazing fat-positive activists and performers like Nomy Lamm and Beth Ditto in the queer community. Being a person who had struggled with eating issues, it really spoke to me that the negative messages I had been receiving my whole life about fat were wrong. I learned that the myths about health and fat were not true and had never been proven in solid scientific studies. I noticed how fatphobic a lot of the world was, and how fatphobic I was too. I realized that the way fat and fat people were treated by society was oppressive and violent. I tried to change my behaviour around fat and stopped vocalizing negative things about it.

When it came to my gender and body, though, I had a block. I thought the way my body had arranged itself was not the way a man's body looked. Even if I could be positive about fat, I thought that my fat was in the wrong spots, and there was little I could do about it. I started lifting weights to try to melt away my chest, lying on my back on an orange vinyl weight bench that I'd found in the basement of the house I lived in. I lifted weights every day. I started running in an attempt to lose weight on my hips, and I often spent a lot of time looking at them in the mirror and wondering if there was some sort of surgery that could make the bones in them smaller. The less support I had as a trans person, the more the urge to change my body would return. I was often reminded by others that they did not see me as a man, which would make me recoil and step back inside my body. Slowly, though, over the course of ten years, I came to accept my decision not to change my voice, and I continued to reap the benefits of being a singer. I tried to be as healthy about my body as I could.

In 2006, when I was twenty-five, I was in Amsterdam when I attended a panel about the laws concerning sexual reassignment that included a discussion of how different countries in the European Union treat the subject. It became clear to me that governments were the ultimate authorities in deciding the legal distinctions between male and female, and in determining the definitions of where one fit within (or outside) the gender binary, including those self-identified as transgender or intersex. In most places, the requirement for changing one's legal sex was full-on sexual reassignment surgery, including procedures that cause sterilization of the reproductive organs. I have always had little respect for institutions, and on that day I swore to no longer think of my gender as a natural or innate thing. I was a person who identified as male, and I should not have to alter my body in any way to prove to the government that I was.

The institutional sterilization of trans people really stood out as a particularly violent act to me, so I decided to research the current laws in Canada. It differed between provinces, but at that time SRSs (sex reassignment surgeries), including sterilizing procedures, were required of people who wanted to legally change their sex. This was news to me. I had ruled out going through the legal process myself because hormone therapies were the first step in the treatment of gender identity disorder, and I didn't want them. I was not surprised by this new information, but it enraged me.

My relationship with my body shifted. I no longer believed in the gender or sex binaries as if they were laws of nature. I was not a man trapped in a woman's body. All I should have had to do to be a man was to say that I was one. The rules of bodies and gender were socialized, not innate. I re-examined my fat politics and tried to take the requirements of the gender binary out of my thinking processes. It all became clearer to me, and, as I started to look more at the men and women I encountered in my everyday life, no one body seemed to be living up to every single one of the stereotypes that gendered bodies were expected to present. It wasn't true that men couldn't have larger chests or hips, or that women had to have them. I saw variations on what was thought to be an ideal body in both men and women on a daily basis. Yet society was telling everyone that their bodies were wrong.

My childhood idea that my body was a spaceship came back to me. I was not in the wrong body. I was in the wrong world. I wished so hard that my body was capable of interstellar travel, but sadly, it's not possible for me to jettison myself outside the world of gender pressure. Even though I still struggle with the pressures of gender and body image issues, I work hard to remember that it's not my body that's the problem. Instead, I try to use that energy to turn my efforts outwards. I refuse to accept that the way my body looks should determine my gender. I refuse to accept that fat is gendered in any arrangement on my body or anyone else's. I refuse to think of fat as unhealthy. It may be a very long time before the way that gender and fat are dealt with changes, but I am the happiest I've ever been in my body, and it has been such a relief to realize that I am no longer living inside the problem.

Messages to Lynn

Ivan: Hey, pal. Love reading your status updates here. You are a true genius. Sorry to hear about your accident today. The pictures of your poor finger looked nasty. Hope the stitches heal up okay. Speaking of stitches, for some reason I felt the need to tell you that after many years of contemplation and general brain wandering about the whole big picture, I finally took a deep breath and had top surgery seven days ago. Whew. No T, and no intentions that way so far, but had to lose the ladies and so I finally did.

I saw my chest for the first time today. They changed the bandages and removed the sewn-on nipple cover thingies, and I saw my body how I have dreamt it in nearly every fantasy I ever had in my whole life, waking or asleep. Bruised and puffy still, and my nipples hanging on for dear life, but even so. There it was. There I was.

Today I was thinking about a conversation we had way back in the day in a park in Seattle on a tour somewhere. I don't recall what either of us said, not a word, really, but something I remember about it only in my heart or animal brain told me to write you and tell you I did it. And now it feels like the light shone on me there today like it maybe never has and I thought you might want to hear this story for some reason. That's all. Hope your finger doesn't hurt too bad and Stay Gold, Ponyboy. I sure do love you from up here in Canada and way down in my belly. My brother.

xoxo,

Ivan

Lynn: Dude stop you made me cry. Always do. Love you. So happy for you. It's poignant isn't it? How we tried to accept and finally had to accept that its losing 'em that is what we really want. So good. I love you! Good healing. I remember that day, pal. Yep.

Oh, P.S. it was an electric hedge trimmer! So we both had some cutting to do this week. Yours is better tho. Do you have drains? Where did you go? I heard the Canadian doc is really great out Toronto way.

Ivan: Yeah I feel like I worked real hard to make space for me to be okay how I am and I was pretty okay considering some days the whole world seems to want to disappear dudes like us and now I have even more okay inside me plus all that space in the world I carved out for myself too. I have drains. Sheer torture, those. I am a little allergic to them it seems, so now I have blisters, too, and scabs from them. They hurt even more than where the doctor's hedge trimmers got me. Seriously. I went to a surgeon here in Vancouver, and I am more than happy so far, but who knows in the long run, I literally change so much every day. I remember when Zena and I got this little apartment and it had a dishwasher and when I first saw it I was all I never had one of those before since I lived on my own, and never needed one, I wash my own dishes what kind of a lazy bastard needs a dishwasher anyways your gran would be ashamed of you right now if she was still here to see you all gone soft for the modern conveniences. But then I fell in love hard. Well that is exactly the same love story I am having with my man nipples right now. There they are, clinging on to me for dear life and I can't even feel the little buggers, like I mean at all, no feeling whatsoever but I never knew how much I would love them looking like this I thought it wouldn't matter but it does and wouldn't you know it I can't raise my arms high enough yet to wash a single fucking plate it hurts to scrub anything and fuck me if I don't love that goddamn dishwasher even more now like it was an electric angel or something.

I hear the surgeon in Toronto somehow does this surgery without having the drains in and well that just seems too good to really be true like some kind of sleight-of-hand from where I sit right now propped up and leaking and sore and itchy eight days in and two more to go and maybe more for the right side of my chest, that tit always was the problem one what with the cysts from binding and that turned-out-not–to-be-cancer scare a couple years back but I also know a real nice fella who had it done last month in Toronto and he looks great. I could put you in touch if you want.

That is all here live from flat and happy chest city. Don't be a stranger and hope that finger heals up nicely. Your comment about don't worry ladies it's the left hand cracked me up dude. You should write a book hey wait you already did and man I can't wait for your next one.

always your brother,

Ivan notits Coyote

Lynn: You're one funny guy. And always with the sweet angle. Brother from another mother. Why don't we spend any time together, are you way out in the woods still? Yeah, hook a brother up with the tit taker from Toronto. No drains. That would be good.

How to Be a Transgender Country Singer

How do you become a transgender country singer? For some, it's easier to be transgender from the start and then work towards becoming a singer. For others, it's better to play music first, and then come out as transgender. About ten years ago, I managed to do both in the space of a few months. Half a year after moving to Vancouver from Alberta, country music started to swirl in my head. I had put all of myself into escaping from Calgary to the more liberal west coast. I had changed my last name a few days before I moved, and I was keen on reinventing myself. I was queer, and that had been hard in Alberta. I thought that I would put those difficulties behind me and wake up a new person in Vancouver, but the temperate climate and easygoing people there had reaffirmed the sense that I was still quite Albertan on the inside. It's not like the moment I put my foot down in British Columbia, I was wholly inspired to start making surfer music. The music that had surrounded me my entire life started to creep into my own. As a kid, I had mostly hated being trapped in the world of Garth Brooks circa the 1990s. My uncles would often break into shorthand versions of "Friends in Low Places" just to annoy me, and so I had never tried to seek out country music on purpose. In Calgary, it was all around me, but in Vancouver I felt a void I hadn't predicted. The twangy voices and toe-tapping cowboy boots began to call to me from across the Rocky Mountains.

One day I was wandering around on Commercial Drive in Vancouver during one of my periods of unemployment, and I walked into a used record store because I saw a glockenspiel in the window. I was thinking that buying one might turn my mood around. The glock ended up being too pricy, but as I started to walk out of the store feeling rather low, a used CD in the racks caught my eye. The fellow on the cover looked about as lonely and defeated as I felt. It was Hank Williams. I bought it and rushed home to my third-floor apartment, putting it in my CD player as soon as I walked through the door. As the sun was sinking gold over the Vancouver skyline, the lonesome howl of Hank Williams and the high-pitched replies of a lap steel guitar called me home. He was almost too twangy for my taste, but he sounded as misplaced as I felt. His music pulled me back to the rural places where my family once lived, and to the city where I grew up. I started to listen to Hank on repeat. After a few months, I started to write more like him. I would sit down with my guitar, imagining the endless roads in the flat expanses of my youth, and I ended up writing songs about the prairies, songs about the dust bowl, songs about trains. Before I knew it, I had written twelve of them. Overnight, and quite accidentally, I had become a country singer.

At the same time as I was writing songs for my first album, I came out as transgender. I had decided that I wanted to live my life as a man. These events happened side by side, but they didn't happen because of each other. They just happened to be two parts of my identity that ended up transforming simultaneously. It was not a great business plan. It was also a bit terrifying when I started planning the promotion of my first album. I was poised to tour across Canada with my new songs. The way that bands from Vancouver toured Canada was to drive from one coast to the other and then back, playing anywhere that would have them. The parts of Canada that had been unfriendly to me as a queer person were now stretched out before me, awaiting my return, this time as a transgender person. I didn't have a lot of expectations of being welcomed. There was no room for people like me where I was from, but still, I was from there. Somehow I would have to manage singing my way back.

I had decided that my outfits should reflect my music and would give me a fighting chance in small towns. I picked up the wardrobe of a country singer with a cowboy hat, belt buckles, cowboy shirts, and, of course, boots. I cut my hair very short so that there was no chance of being perceived as ambiguously gendered. I practiced my swagger and kicking dust with my boots. I was ready.

The first parts of the tour were in British Columbia: Vancouver, Nelson, Kelowna, and Cranbrook. Everything went okay: there was a lot of misgendering, but no physical threats. Late on the fifth afternoon, the van roared into Alberta. Red Deer was my first small-town prairie test. I pulled up outside of a bar in the bright spring afternoon and walked in. As my eyes adjusted to the light, my blood pressure rose. The regulars gave me a lazy once-over in my over-the-top cowboy outfit. They probably figured out that I didn't have a real job, and so they turned back to their drinks. There wasn't a speck of mud on my get-up. I went up to the bar just as the bartender blew some fire out of his mouth in a showy move. That shook me up even more, but I managed to say, "Hi, I'm playing here tonight. I was wondering who I should talk to."

"Who wants to know!" a scraggly-looking guy with long hair shouted at me from the other end of the bar.

Uh oh, I thought, looking behind me to see that there was still a path to the door.

"Don't mind Stan," the scraggly guy said, gesturing at the bartender, who then grinned. "He's just training up for a fancier bar with those tricks." He got up from his stool and walked over to me. "I'm Jerry. I own the place. You must be the band?"

"Yep," I said, trying to fake a strong handshake and wishing there was more of me.

After soundcheck, Jerry generously provided me with a dinner of buffalo wings and fries. At least the food was to my liking. Over the next hour or so, the crowd thickened with people who had just gotten off work and were looking for their Friday night fun. Finally Jerry came over and asked, "Are you ready?" I got up onstage and looked out at the crowd, some of whom turned away from their conversations to look at me. I was worried that they would think there was something off about me. That someone would throw a bottle as soon as I opened my mouth. I took a really long time to tune my guitar and banjo, delaying the inevitable. I played a long intro on the guitar before launching into the yodelling part of "Long Gone Lonesome Blues." I think I even winced a little, but as soon as I started singing, a hushed calm spread throughout the bar, and at the end of the song there was some clapping and even one muffled hoot. A lot of the people at the bar looked like members of my family who lived around the area, and when I stepped down from the stage for the break, I realized that one of them was, in fact, my cousin.

He ran a welding shop and was supposed to work that

night, but he left his staff on their own so he could come to the show. In between sets, I asked him about fighting at bars in Red Deer. Earlier, I had heard a rumour that someone just down the block had been stabbed the night before. I was supposed to sleep in a room above the bar that night. I asked, "Do people fight here for drugs or mostly for the hell of it?"

He cocked his head and answered me with a grin. "It doesn't take a reason, really."

A few shows later, I did get into my own irrational fight. It was in Jasper, a mountain town west of Edmonton. I had been playing a festival there that weekend, and afterwards was drinking in the bar with a couple of guys I knew, killing time before having to drive to Edmonton. I had walked out of the washroom and accidentally brushed the arm of a woman who had her back to me. She turned around quickly with narrowed eyes, and said, "Watch where you're going, dyke bitch!"

I knew better than to stay within arm's length of her and walked quickly back to my friends. A couple of minutes later, a few of her friends came over to where we were standing. One of them said to me, "Hey, we saw you play at the festival today. It was awesome." And then another one chimed in with, "Don't mind our friend. She's pregnant, so you shouldn't fight her. I went crazy when I was pregnant too."

I attempted to say something, but nothing came out. I was trying to understand the connection between the pregnancy and the homophobia. They took that as a cue that I wasn't going to make anything out of it and left.

As I worked my way across the rest of Canada, I did my best to avoid any situation that might turn into a fight. Canada is big, and it's made bigger by stopping in almost every town along the way. By the time I got to Toronto, I was elated to be in a big city. I had started to learn how to really get a crowd going in the small-town bars, and I had gained a little confidence. But the show in Toronto was in a queer space, and to my surprise people just stood in front of me as they listened, with their arms crossed. There was no hooting and no boot-stomping. I realized then that it was going to be hard selling country music to queer people, and hard to sell queerness to country people. However, I'd become very attached to my new style of music and decided to do whatever it took to keep playing it. With barriers on both sides, I kept doing a mix of country shows and queer shows. One weekend I'd be at a big city's Pride celebration performing for crowds of gay men in buttless chaps, and the next weekend I'd be playing on a family's farm for prairie folk kicking back in lawn chairs. I can't say that having people refer to me by the right pronoun was more consistent in either of these spaces. People seemed to enjoy my music, but I was feeling that my gender was invisible and disrespected most of the time, even by people I worked with.

One day I was standing by the side of the highway in B.C., hitchhiking with a guy I used to sing country duets with. I sang all of the parts that Dolly Parton or Tammy Wynette would have sung, without calling it much into question. I wasn't an insecure guy, and those were great parts for my voice. I thought my friend knew that we were both Kenny Rogers on the inside, that he believed that I was also a man. We had been stumbling from bar to bar together with our guitars together for a couple of years by then. That day, neither of us had slept, and we stood with our thumbs out watching a river of cars pass us by. We were tired and hungry. I can't remember what I said to him. I'm sure it wasn't kind, because he reached deep in his pocket for his response and pulled out something I didn't even know he had in there.

"You know what your problem is?" he said. "You have penis envy."

It was enough to tear him out of my heart. After we failed at hitchhiking that day, we had only enough money for one Greyhound ticket, and when I got on the bus I knew that the days of me being the Dolly Parton to his Kenny Rogers were over. I knew what he really thought of me. And I knew that I had every right to identify as male without having to change my body. This was when I decided to remove people who didn't allow me this from my life.

Still, I was stubborn. I chose to keep playing everywhere that country singers who weren't transgender were playing. I gained some momentum, using my singing voice as best I could to cross barriers that I couldn't talk my way across. I was even getting known a bit on the country circuit, but the barriers were always apparent. A few of the more famous country singers promised to take me on tour sometime, but never did. I became anxious, wondering if they had heard my music before they knew I was transgender and now would never get around to actually inviting me. I had to play more than two hundred shows a year to keep from having to work a day job, and I could have used their support. There was no way for me to gauge what was just "the music business" and what was actual discrimination.

After five years of constant touring, a friend asked me about gigs in the prairies and if I could recommend some venues. When I asked her what kind of places she'd like to play, she answered, "Anywhere not too sexist or homophobic." I racked my brains and could only come up with a handful of suggestions. Then I thought, why would I keep playing places that I would never send a friend? I realized that I had been very unkind to myself. Playing those places had forced me to censor myself in some of the songs I wrote, because any obvious queerness would have outed me in unsafe situations. I resented the places I played for that.

A few weeks later at a festival in northern Alberta, I ran into one of the famous country singers who had reneged on his promise to take me on tour even though he had taken almost every other act I knew. He pretended he didn't know me and then referred to me as "she." The following weekend, I played a small-town bar in Twin Butte, Alberta. It was sometime around Valentine's Day, and they had decorated a glass gun rack with shiny red hearts and my poster. The sight of my face smiling in front a bunch of guns with hearts all around it was too much. I knew that my songs were welcome in the world of country music, but my gender was not and might never be.

It isn't that I hate country music now, or that I'm not grateful to any of the kind people who gave me a chance to play it by booking me or showing up at shows. I'm happy that I spent time learning about where my family is from, and I got to meet many people I never would have met if I had holed myself up in Vancouver or flown right over to Toronto. I don't think that big cities are synonymous with trans acceptance. I still have faith that there are people who relate to my music no matter where they live. I simply no longer confine the lyrics in my music or the way I dress or behave to conform with the gender binary, and I expect the spaces I play to accept that. I don't think it's too much to ask.

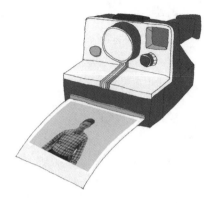

*F*or the first couple of weeks, I couldn't get over my own heart beating. It just seemed so…right there. For the first month or so after surgery, especially. My heart, right there, under my skin, barely covered, hardly protected. Whenever I sang, or walked up a flight of stairs, anything that raised my heart rate even a little, I could see it thumping, right through my T-shirt. I would watch it pulse, kind of alarmed at how vulnerable my own heart suddenly seemed, without its armour. Without its breastplate. My heart. Barely hidden by this skin.

Before, to hurt me, you would have had to stab so much deeper than now.

Invested

Twenty-four days ago, I had top surgery. Technically speaking, this means I had a full bilateral mastectomy with areolar or nipple grafts.

I am a storyteller. Have been for over twenty years now, and this story, the story of me and my chest, is for me the scariest story I have ever written down, by far. But I have been taking deep breaths and writing it. I have and continue to write about this whole crazy journey, all of that jumping through all of those hoops held up by the mostly cisgendered people who make most of the decisions and diagnoses that someone decided needed to be made before I could go ahead and do what I needed to do to live in the body I wanted to live in.

A couple of months before my surgery, I decided that it, and my recovery, were going to be private matters. I decided that I simply did not have it in me to heal and deal at the same time. I did not tell most of my family about it, and I made no mention of my surgery date, the operation itself, or any news of my recovery and adjustment to my new body on Facebook or any other form of social media. As a writer and performer, I live a very public life, but I had no interest at all in my body or my choices becoming a site for public debate. It was important for me to focus on healing. I couldn't even fathom responding to sympathy from strangers, or the inevitable and inexplicably infuriating, though surely well-meant, *hugz* from people who purposely misspell "hugs," not to mention some kinds of second-wave feminist backlash or criticism from readers who have more of an investment in my being female than I currently do. I told only my friends, intimates, collaborators, and my band and choir mates. I planned to write my family a long and carefully crafted letter after the fact, when I was well enough to juggle their and my emotions, and gracefully navigate any questions or fallout.

Exactly one week before I was scheduled for surgery, CBC radio aired a national primetime segment called "The Disappearing Butch?" which debated whether or not butches were being swallowed up by greater access to funded medical transitioning and hormone treatment. One of the interviewees included a shout-out to me as an old-school butch who was not transitioning, and the CBC linked to one of my columns on their web page. My elementary school boyfriend from the Yukon, who I shared a first kiss with halfway up a pine tree in grade four, immediately emailed me to congratulate me on my strength and perseverance. I bit my tongue and counted down the remaining days I had left before I disappeared part of myself.

Three days post-op, I was flat on my back in bed, surfing Percocet and Facebook simultaneously, when I saw a picture that made my heart jump into my throat like a smooth, hot stone. It was a picture of a young trans guy I had met in passing a couple of times. He was sitting up in a hospital bed, wearing the same post-operative compression vest I currently had on. He had obviously just come out of the OR, having just had his very own bilateral radical mastectomy and areolar grafts. But that is not what moved me. What choked me up was that his father was there with him, pictured bending over his son and kissing the soft top of his recently shorn head.

I hadn't even breathed a word of what I was going through to my own father.

I followed this fellow's recovery with great interest. His name is Jessie. A couple of days later, Jessie posted a beautifully executed self-portrait; with his compression vest unhooked and unzipped, revealing the blood-soaked bandages underneath, sneaking a peek at his new chest.

I had snuck the very same peek myself, the night before. I fired off a message to him, telling him I was keeping my news private, but that I had undergone the same surgery with the same surgeon just three days before he had, and that I was really enjoying having a cyber surgery recovery partner, and that I loved his photographs. He wrote me back almost immediately, saying that he had seen my and Rae Spoon's *Gender Failure* show last spring, including a piece I do about going to the shrink's office to get a mental health assessment prior to my surgery being funded, and that he recalled thinking at the time that we both seemed to be pretty close together on The List, waiting for a date for surgery. He asked how I was, then he wrote a bit about his recovery and how he was feeling about it all, and then he added a postscript: *P.S. I don't know if this connection was ever made, but if not, I figure you'd appreciate the backstory.*

He included a link to a column of mine, dated April of 2009, which was a story about a woman I had met when I was taking a bag of clothes out to my truck to donate them. The woman had been unloading a bunch of cleaning supplies and a vacuum out of a small hatchback, and my little dog had bounded over to her and put his head in her lap when she knelt to pet him. She told me how sweet he was, and I bragged that he was a gifted therapy pet, that my dog sitter took him to visit a home for people with Alzheimer's, and that he was a big hit there.

"You should take him into the cancer ward," she told me. "They would love him there. He really is a special guy, I can tell. They could use him there. I should know." Her eyes met mine. "I've just come through my third battle with cancer myself."

I knew I had seen that haircut before. My friend Carole from Ottawa, most recently. The short, short hair of a woman who recently had none at all.

Then she stood up, wiped her hands on her pants, and turned to pick up the vacuum cleaner and a milk crate full of cleaning supplies.

"You moving in?" I asked her. "You need a hand with that stuff?"

She shook her head. "I'm the housecleaner. I work for the real estate company."

I looked down at the Pine Sol, the Windex, Pledge, ammonia, bleach. All those chemicals, I thought.

"You back at work already?" I asked, the question sounding stupid before it had even fully left my mouth.

She smiled soft and patient at me. "Cancer doesn't care how the rent gets paid."

I nodded, and she started to head toward the stairs of the recently renovated and flipped heritage house. I took a few steps toward my truck, and for some reason turned back to her and said: "You wouldn't happen to know anyone who needs some clothes, would you? They're all clean and in good

142

condition. Men's clothes," I told her. "Shirts and ties and stuff. I just thought maybe you might know someone who could use them."

Her eyes lit up. "Someone like my eighteen-year-old transgender son?" She reached out a thin arm to take the bag from me.

I smiled wide. "Yeah, someone just like that. That would be just about perfect."

She opened the bag, and closed it again.

"He just came out to me recently. He will love this. We can't afford a whole new wardrobe right now."

The column ended with her and I giving each other a full-body, random-stranger-on-a- street-corner hug, and then going our separate ways.

About a year ago someone wrote to me to let me know that the woman in the column had passed away. Everybody called her Blue, on account of the striking cerulean colour of her eyes.

I re-read the column again, and then read the rest of Jessie's message, all the pieces clicking in my head like Lego bits.

"So I was that freshly-out trans kid that got your old clothes," Jessie wrote. "And the woman you met that day was my mother, who just passed away June 22nd last year. She'd been planning on being the one to take care of me during my surgery recovery, but at least she got to help me lay down the framework of my boyhood for a few years.

"Thanks for the hand-me-downs! It's not fucking easy finding a good queer-sized button-down."

Jessie and I have since done a photo shoot together, wearing nothing but our vests and neckties, our blood-filled surgical drains dangling and pinned to our hips, like gun holsters. We text or call each other almost every day, with excited updates and nipple questions and crusty and scabby complaints. I bring him vitamins and offer unsolicited and possibly non-consensual dating advice. I am twice his age, almost exactly.

A couple of days ago, Jessie sent me a picture of himself taken a few years back, with his birth father in Toronto, wearing one of the shirts I had given his mother on the street that day. His father looks, well, about my age, and Jessie looks impossibly young, and sweet, and handsome. And from the shape of his jaw in the photograph, it looks like he had not yet started taking testosterone. I don't know if he ever identified as butch before he transitioned. He hasn't ever asked me if I still do. Funny enough, it hasn't even come up.

YouTube Gender

In January of 2008, I heard about a new website that allowed people to post videos of themselves online for the world to see. I was feeling a bit cut off from my own world because at the time I was living in a small town in Germany. I decided to record a video of myself singing in my share house and upload it to YouTube. In the video my hair was in an untamed mullet because I didn't know how to speak German, and I was too nervous to go to the only salon in town because its name was Hair Killer. I was wearing oversize wire-framed glasses from the 1970s, and there was a rack of my laundry drying behind me. I performed an acoustic version of a brand new song I had written called "Come On Forest Fire Burn the Disco Down," about the ongoing colonialism in Canada. The song is a series of questions asked of people who, like myself, fall in the category of benefiting vastly from the history of Canada being a colony. I was nervous about the song and had rewritten it over fifty times. I thought that posting it would get me some valuable feedback from the public. The video appeared with the description: "Acoustic version of

147

new song recorded in Weimar, Germany, January 2008."

I had always been an independent musician and for the most part sheltered from public opinion about myself due to my lack of mainstream media attention. I knew that I didn't project the typical image of a male-identified musician, but I thought that performers like Prince had paved the way for my high-pitched voice decades earlier. To my surprise, there was an unexpected landslide of opinions posted about my video. What follows is a list of all the comments that viewers posted that had anything to do with my gender, appearance, or voice. Some of them are hidden from public view because they got too many thumbs down on the site. I think that taken together, they read as a poem of sorts about gender expectations in the music industry.

"boy or girl? :)"

"are you a chick?"

"Rae Spoon has a vagina."

"Hello Mr. Rae Spoon, will you marry me? :) I wanna live in Weimar with you. <3 Much love!!!"

"are you a boy or a girl?"

"i think he is a boy..but he or she is very ugly"

"nice voice but what is up with your hair"

"For a canadian transgender, Rae Spoon is an amazing singer/ songwriter."

"androgyny sessions."

Rae

"Guy or girl…"

"did he make this song?? Its really good. i like his voice as well!"

"dude that was fucking remarkable you remind me of a young Neil Young"

"wow man! that is really great! you have tons of talent!"

"wtf u sound like a girl .. =="

"awkward……. I think she is……."

"even more awkward…he's not…"

"wow you are like a new Fiest or something you make me think of fiest mixed with amy milan broken social scene should pick you up haha nice work watch out for too much vibratto, by the way"

"HOLY SHIT DUDE YOU'RE A CHICK!!!!"

"I'm a young man and I know you probably love women but I would like to lay in a bed and just talk with you, you seem amazing , lovelovelove"

"at first i thought this was a joke and then you started to sing. i would like to say this song is really good. did you write it yourself?"

"you are a guy or a girl?"

"you have a great voice but grow out your hair and lose the glasses and you'll look much better =] "

"yeah, someone's gender and sexuality is their own business, the song is amazing you said that, everything else is pointless."

"girl right?"

"I'm just pretending it's a girl the voice is great anyways, and the guy/ gal is pretty cute :]"

"a bird or a lad? who knows? Awful haircut anyway."

"you look the dude from into the wild if he were to make it another month or so, but sound kinda like laura veirs"

"Wholy SHIT woman! Your voice is BEAUTIFUL, move over Kerry Underword, ect."

"good song. but i just dont see you on tv. you look like someone from wonder years. but hey youre still awesome! peace."

"Great voice girl, you have to look more like a girl if you want to succed. Thats how the world is :-/ "

"A GIRL???? i know LOL. I was wondering the same thing myself"

"was expecting myself to laugh at this video, but this is pretty good :o"

"Dude- wtf? He's so hot. Not everyone has to look the same."

"well she's a girl"

"wow, is this original? you could go far … granted if you changed your hair and got contacts. (:"

"Yeah , it sounds great! Like the woman of the cranberries ^^"

"are you a dude or a chick?"

"youre the first person ive seen who has a mullet and large glasses and some how pulls it off. ...thats a compliment. sweet song"

"a woman, or very geeky man?"

"WHAT GENDER ARE YOU?!?!?!?! pretty good vid though btw. thumbs up."

"Is this … a man? A woman?"

"Why did you steal my grandfather's glasses?"

"Are you a girl?"

"Who are you?"

Dear Family

July 8, 2013

My Dearest Family:

I have been thinking about writing this letter for over a month now, so here I finally go.

On June 3rd I had a radical double mastectomy. I am fine, and healthy, and to allay your worst fears, I do not have cancer. I chose this, after over twenty years of thinking about it and considering all the implications. I am now five weeks post-operative, and I go in for my latest check-up this Thursday, where I expect the surgeon will tell me more of what he has been telling me so far: that I am healing very well, and that there have been no complications.

Maybe some of you are wondering, "So what?" or thinking, "Whoa, too much information," and I must admit I did consider keeping this news to myself, but after thinking carefully and at length about it, I have decided to be as honest and open about it as I can possibly be, mostly because I love you and I want to include you in the important things in my life, and this decision counts as a life-changing one for me.

Remember way back in the late eighties when I appeared on the evening news sliding down a flag pole, after replacing the Canadian flag with a rainbow flag, into the waiting arms of the Vancouver Police Department? That was how I came out of the closet to a lot of you, and I feel bad about that to this day. I regret that I was too young and silly to have taken the time to sit down with you all one by one and respectfully and thoughtfully come out to you, and tell you about my life, and give you the respect and space you deserved to ask me questions and process it all. It is easy enough to blame that on the folly of youth, but now, at nearly forty-four years of age, I think I can do better by you.

So here goes: It is probably not much of a surprise to any of you that I possess a not-so-typical gender identity. I am not currently taking nor do I plan to take testosterone and "transition" to male, but for many years I have been living with an increasing amount of discomfort in my body, specifically around the ever-increasing size of my breasts. You guys, like most of the world, don't know this about me, because I was binding them down for the last nineteen years, but I was a size 42D. That is not a typo. 42D. Suffice it to say I did not take after the Daws side of the family in the boobs department. Binding them down was increasingly uncomfortable and unhealthy, especially during the summer and at the gym, or choir practice, and while playing the saxophone, and as of the last three years or so I have been experiencing numbness and tingling in three fingers on my left hand, and suffering from pain in my neck and shoulders. It was time. Even though I am still recovering, and stiff and sore and only starting to regain my energy levels, I can say already that it was the right decision for me. I am happier in my body than I remember being since I was twelve years old or so, and I have taken to calling my clothes closet The Joy Factory. I feel lighter. About six pounds lighter, as it turns out.

As I write this, I can't believe I am talking about my tits to my uncles and aunts and cousins and parents and grandmother. But I don't want any of you to find out through Facebook, or rumour, or in my next book, or to see me in person and wonder but not know for sure, and for any of you to think that I don't love or trust you enough to be honest and if you will pardon the pun, keep you abreast of this development. I want you to know that you are receiving this letter because you are important to me and I am taking this as my second chance to come out to you.

I know this may be hard for some of you to understand. It took me years to come to this decision, and to make it right in my own head and heart. If you have any questions or thoughts, please feel free to share them with me. I promise to answer them with all of the compassion and understanding you have always blessed me with.

I love you always.

Ivan

● ● ●

I sent this letter to my entire huge family, those with Internet access, anyway, at about 5 o'clock on a Tuesday night, I think it was. As soon as I hit send, I felt a little nauseous. I know my family, and they are good people, but still. I am, as far as I know, the first trans person any of them know up close and personal. Most of what they know was probably gleaned from Jerry Springer, or something of the like. The first email response arrived in my inbox about two hours later, from my grandmother, typing away on her iPad from the couch, probably wearing a flowered house dress with her legs tucked up under her bum like she does. She is ninety-four years old, and her email was two lines long, with the single word "boobs" in the subject line. It read:

> *I wish I could get rid of mine. You could wave goodbye with them.*
> *Love, see you soon*
>
> *Grandma Pat*

Then came this, from my one of my aunts:

> *It's always good to hear from you. Thanks for being so open about your surgery, I'm sure you did a lot of soul-searching before making that big decision. Remember that Uncle Rob and I are very proud of you and the choices that you have made in your life and know it hasn't always been easy for you. We love you and will always respect any decisions that you and Zena make. I hope you are feeling happy and healthy now. Take care and give each other a big hug and kiss from us.*
>
> *Love you both! Love, Aunt Cathy and Uncle Rob*

Then this from my cousin who was too young to understand how much I botched my original coming out:

Nobody has ever shared with me how you came out, I never asked and nobody ever had to tell me. I suppose this is because I have only ever known you as Ivan and questions weren't necessary. I have always loved you for you. I had a gulp in my throat while reading your letter, thank you for sharing your experience with me.
xo Lindsey

I got this missive from another of my cousins, sent from the backstage of the nightclub where she is currently working as a dancer, at least until she can finish her dental hygienist's program at night school:

Hi hunny, that was a very surprising email, and to be honest with you, I wish I read it at a more appropriate time, as I'm working and wish I could give you a more lengthy response about how amazing I think you are. I will tomorrow. But for now ... I'll thank you soo much for being so brave and honest with all of us. And I respect any decision you need to make for YOUR life. I never judged you before, and I never will. You are one of the most influential people in my life, whether you know it or not, and I love you soo much. I have to get going, but will check in with you tomorrow. I love you and I know you will be ok.

Hi again! I'm back, I have some time and re-read ur email. I must also say, on a lighter note, 42 D?!!!! WTF ... It's a little funny to me, that what I paid $8000 for 3 different times, you wanted nothing to do with! Lol!! This just proves that everything has a different importance and meaning to every individual. And seriously

GOOD for you for being so upfront, this really saves
from the not so subtle, questioning, sometimes judg-
mental looks I sometimes receive! Haha!! Good!!! And
I feel you on the weight and back problems! It takes a
toll that's for sure!! Well... You have been through an
amazing journey and I'm proud of you!! You are truly a
remarkable person!! Love you again!!

Racheal

And this, from another of my many cousins:

Got your email. Happy for you. Glad you're healthy and
happy. Can you eat Vietnamese chicken wings any faster
now? Just wondering.

Ryan

My dad called me on the phone, after his wife had read him
my letter, in keeping with his "Why would I want to learn
how to use a computer?" approach to life. He said, and I do
quote: "First of all, I just have to say that if I had to strap my
nuts down to go out of the house, they'd have been gone years
ago." He paused for me to laugh, like a seasoned stand-up
would. "And I guess it's pretty brave to write everybody, but
you didn't have to. As far as I'm concerned, it's all none of
their fucking business. It's your body. If I wanted to cut my
dick off, I shouldn't have to answer to anyone for that. My
dick, my decision. I mean, there would be a lot of disappointed
females out there, but that wouldn't be my responsibility."

So. That all went even better than I had hoped.

*L*ittle girl about four years old in the elevator asks me: "Why you have tattoos all over yourself? You look like a mean man." I smile at her. "Oh, okay," she adds, "not when you are smiling. Guess what? We are having pizza for dinner. Guess why? Because Daddy can only cook breakfast things." Her mom and I then crack right up.

How to Be a Transgender Indie Rocker

I was walking down the dark streets of Weimar in Germany. I had only been there for a couple of days after joining my girlfriend who was just starting an art school program there. We were on our way to a venue called Planbar to meet some students from the art school. I could hear our footsteps echoing off of the tall sandstone buildings with graffiti and broken windows as I tried to verify with my girlfriend that the people we were about to meet knew that I was trans.

"Yeah. I told them that you're trans and to call you 'he.' They seemed to understand," she replied. "We'll see."

I didn't know very many people in Weimar, let alone in Germany. I had recently quit drinking for the second time and was not feeling as numb to wrong pronouns as I had been when I could have a couple of drinks. Also, I didn't really know the first thing about professional art. I had even thought that the shortening of the Museum of Modern Art in Manhattan, MoMA, was a French word when my girlfriend had once told me to meet her there. I was probably going to end up offending some of the art people as much as they offended me.

Here goes nothing, I thought to myself as I pushed open the heavy old door of the bar, wondering if I'd made a huge mistake moving to a new continent for love. A few students were already there, gathered around a large wooden table, so we pulled up aluminum chairs and joined them.

After the introductions, I settled back with my cola and let the first few wrong pronouns wash over me. I wasn't feeling like I wanted to correct anyone, and I tried to remain as quiet as possible. It was loud, and the smoke in the room grew thick as more students joined us. The person to my left was introduced as Alex, a partner of one of the other students. That was the first thing we had in common. I shifted my posture to face him a little more.

"What do you do?" I asked him while others at the table started talking about art stuff.

"I run music programs for youth, and sometimes sound installations for galleries," he replied. "And you?"

"I'm a folk singer," I said.

"What is that?" he asked, looking at me like he was genuinely interested.

"Well." I paused. "I suppose that folk music is the music of the people. The expression of organic songs indicative of the time. Ummm. Actually, maybe hip hop is folk music now too... Never mind. I guess I play the acoustic guitar and sing country music."

"Interesting," he replied. "Based on that description, I think that the folk music right now in Germany must be techno."

"Really?" I asked. I wondered to myself: Wasn't techno a dead-sounding, repetitive, computer-generated genre? What was so hard about making music on the computer? It couldn't involve as much skill as learning to, say, sing or play the guitar.

"Yes," Alex replied, more passionately than I'd expected. "It was something that was just getting big when I was a teenager. The techno rave scene. Most German teenagers were expressing themselves with electronic music in the 1990s instead of electric guitars. It was a sound that just grew out of nowhere. Right where we lived. I went to music school in Liverpool when I was older. People at my school would be showing off playing guitar solos by leaping from fret to fret while I invented my own instruments and made music by doing the tiniest movements. I tried to learn how to play electric guitar like one of the Beatles, but it was the small ticks of minimal techno that really stuck with me. Maybe it will wear off on you being here?"

And it did. It started out with a cracked copy of Ableton Live software, version four, and my very first computer that I found on Craigslist in Berlin. Alex gave me the program and showed me how all synthesizers were built from oscillating waves. He showed me how to build my own drum sounds from scratch. I began to understand that computers were instruments too, and infinitely more complex than I assumed. They had the capability to hold and manipulate the sounds from other instruments and audio waves. I locked myself in my room with my slow-running computer and tried to use the tools he gave me to write songs.

The months wore on in Weimar and I started to change to better match my surroundings. After managing to extricate myself from the Canadian prairies, I realized that I did, in fact, continue to exist outside of them. I began replacing my cowboy clothing for tight black jeans and fluorescent t-shirts. In the former East German tower-block housing I lived in, writing about the open sky started to feel a bit disingenuous. My career as a transgender country singer had been full of painful moments, mostly because of my gender. I wasn't feeling very loyal to the genre I had spent so much time developing. I had thought I was going to be a country singer forever, but my head began to turn toward instruments that used electricity and computer chips. That's the moment I found electronic music and indie rock. By the time I moved back to Canada two years later, I had all of the blips and bleeps and synth sounds that Germany had to offer.

I moved to Montreal and released all of my experiments on a new album. I wasn't sure how to market myself as an ex-cowboy, but I went with glamourizing my departure from country music and my time hiding out in Germany. I started my tour in Kitchener, Ontario, and a friend of mine there who had always come out to my country music shows, at least when he wasn't off for hunting season, came. In the break between sets, he pulled on my arm and said, "Rae, you got weird in Europe, eh?"

I paused, and then brought up the last time I was in town. "You think I'm weird? Weren't you the guy who'd had a dead deer in the back of his truck for two weeks the last time I was here?"

"Yeah," he said, "but it was winter, so it was frozen. Same thing as stuffing it in my freezer. Anyways, your music got weird, but I still like it."

The gender and genre rules of the country music industry had been strict, but luckily by already breaking one set of rules, the audiences who came to my shows seemed ready to let me break others. There was no indie rock equivalent to the song "Stand By Your Man" or "Man, I Feel Like a Woman." A lot of the time I couldn't make out what the lyrics to songs by the weird new bands were. They didn't seem to be singing anything about men or women. Maybe this was going to change everything for me. Maybe it was the part of the music industry that was going to make space for my music and overlook the oddity of my variant gender.

However, fleeing the construct of genre turned out not to include freedom from the constructs of gender. I started to see the same patterns in the indie rock scene that I saw in country music. There were very few women in bands, very few slots at festivals for bands with women in them, and there was the same lack of space for people of colour in general. There were also the same kinds of practical problems, like the sound guys who assumed I didn't know how to run my ten guitar pedals, and the all-dude bands playing after me who stepped all over my gear as they set up instead of giving me even a moment to clear off the stage. There was the same worry from promoters that I wasn't marketable, and there was the same amount of friction and tension I felt being a trans person in the music industry.

There are many musicians who are affected by these issues. I am certainly not alone. I guess my point is that alternative venues are not automatically the most supportive. The freedom that is part of the rhetoric about indie music has long been commercialized, and that freedom is reserved only for certain people.

At the pinnacle of the indie rock experience is the hipster festival. I was excited when I started getting invited to play at these events. I like meeting a lot of musicians and seeing a lot of acts. At my first festival, I noticed that the four-star hotel where many musicians were staying was full of clientele who might usually be considered underdressed. Most of them I perceived as cisgender white men between the ages of twenty and thirty-five. I saw some amazing bands at that festival and I genuinely enjoyed playing my sets there, but the hotel was like a scene from *Lord of the Flies*, with a slightly older cast.

On the second morning of the festival, I was in the elevator and a boy got in with an unlit cigarette hanging out of his mouth. I guess he was headed outside to smoke. I thought he was wearing green shoes, but when I looked closer I realized he was only wearing a pair of holey green socks. For some reason this upset me, but at first I couldn't figure out why. After that encounter, I couldn't turn anywhere without noticing the anarchy that being an indie rocker affords young men. They were running around in packs as if social rules didn't apply to them. They were swimming in the pool in their underwear and bobbing for apples in the whirlpool. I'm all for personal freedom when it's for everyone, but not when it's only for musicians staying in a fancy hotel, especially when their rudeness affects the hotel workers working nine-to-five jobs—the very people who supported those musicians in the first place.

I'm not going to say that I wasn't one of those boys selected by the hipster festival and staying at the hotel, but I will say that I am done trying to find a genre of commercial music that will accept my gender. Instead, I have been focusing on the spaces that are accepting of me and trying to find ways to extend that as much as possible to others in the same position.

A Cautionary Tale

I've heard a couple versions of the following story, but the gist of it happens like this: one of my uncles was driving his truck home one night after a couple of after-work beers with the boys in town. It was the dead of a Yukon winter, dark and black ice all around and cold, but not real cold like it can get. Like maybe minus ten or fifteen. This detail will quickly become an important one. If had been colder out that night, this story might have a very different ending.

The story goes like this: he was driving through the dark and fiddling with the satellite radio in his truck, that's the last thing he remembers. Next thing is he is waking up, and somehow he is stretched out on the hood of his own truck, his head and one arm and shoulder stuck through the windshield, which has been popped right out of its frame. He is wearing his own windshield around his neck like a portable stockade, and there is sticky blood in his hair. He struggles to pull his head and arm out, and a breathtaking shot of pain explodes out of his shoulder. His arm is dislocated. He grits his teeth and rips himself free with his still-good arm, and then forces himself to shrug the shoulder attached to his dangling arm and shock it back into its socket. He passes out from the pain in the snow for an undetermined period of time. When he comes to for the second time, his teeth are chattering and he can't feel his toes. His truck is fifty feet off the highway, crunched into a sturdy jack pine, stalled right next to a steep cliff that falls away sharp into the frozen river below. Everything is now covered in a light dusting of snow that almost blankets the shattered glass and blood and the spot where he doesn't remember throwing up the beer and peanuts he ingested at the bar just before he headed home.

He manages to haul himself up the hill and through the ditch to the edge of the highway, his work boots crunching through the drifting snow that's melting in his wool socks and soaking the cuffs of his jeans. He hitches a ride home with two ladies in a hatchback, who repeatedly offer to turn the car around and drive him back into town to the hospital to get the gash in his head looked at, which he insists is not necessary. Once home, he passes out on his couch with a bag of frozen peas melting in his good hand.

First thing the next morning, he calls my dad, because my dad has a big winch bolted onto the front bumper of his Ford F-150 pick-up. My father comes and gets my uncle, a thermos of black tea with canned milk and sugar and an extra tin camping mug rolling around on the bench seat between them as they drive back to the scene of the accident. My dad pulls his truck over, flicks on the emergency flashers, and surveys the now almost invisible tire tracks that lead off the highway and skirt the sheer drop-off to the now still river. Their breath makes little clouds in the cold blue morning. Everything is white-covered and quiet. A raven squawks through the silence from somewhere. My dad shakes his head, and then crunches back through the snow to hook the winch to the bumper of my uncle's truck and haul it back up to the highway. He doesn't ask a lot of questions. The truck suffered a small dent on the front bumper and needed a new windshield, and my uncle suffered from a sore arm and a scabby head for a couple weeks, and the incident was quickly put in the past.

I hear the story from another one of my uncles, and a slightly different account from my dad. I recount the tale to my sweetheart that evening in bed. My wife is the assistant director of a research institute that focuses on gender and health. She shakes her head at me.

"You sound proud of him." She sounds not so proud of me that I sound proud of him.

I admit that I kind of am. "It's pretty butch to pop your own dislocated arm back into its socket with no help from anyone," I explain.

She harumphs and narrows her eyes at me. "I would highly recommend that you not hold up the men in your family as positive role models when it comes to health care. Remember what I was telling you about hegemonic masculinity and its impact on men's health behaviour? Not advisable."

She is definitely not kidding.

I should tell you here that my wife grew up in her own frozen northern town, raised by a single mom on welfare. She tells me this not because she doesn't get where I come from, but because she knows exactly too well; her own Thunder Bay good old boys looming large in her rear-view mirror.

I think about this story a lot as I heal from top surgery. I come up with my own term for my own version of removing my own windshield from around my own neck with my own one good arm. Cowboying it up, I call it, and every time I consider doing something stubborn and counter to the surgeon's instructions, I remind myself not to cowboy it up. Don't climb up on a chair to get the toaster down, all bandaged up and high on Percocet. Don't play the tenor saxophone ten days after a double mastectomy. Don't take out your own stitches. Ask for help reaching for the frozen gluten-free bread, even if you do have to make up a lie to the lady who asks what kind of surgery you just had and you end up lying about a torn rotator cuff for ten minutes, which you know nothing about whatsoever and which she herself is actually recovering from in real life. Cowboy it down, cowboy. I run through the list of cautionary post-top-surgery tales in my head: my friend in Portland who popped a stitch because he decided he needed to dig up a yucca plant from his garden. My buddy in Halifax who might need a surgical revision now because he blew a stitch when he broke down and vacuumed the rug on his own because the dog hair was taking over his life.

At my one-month post-op check-up, the surgeon lets out a low whistle and tells me that I look like I am two months healed up.

"It's because I am cowboying it down," I inform him, and he knits his eyebrows together in confusion.

"I am no longer looking to the men in my family as role models for my approach to health care," I explain. I don't think he gets it. He is a fancy plastic surgeon in his tenth-floor office overlooking the big city. Why would he?

Later, in the truck, I note the irony that in order to heal properly from having a significant part of my female self removed from the flesh of me, I have to unlearn exactly what all the men in my family would have done.

How to Be Gay When the Gays Won't Have You

Eight years ago, I was standing outside of the Vauxhall Tavern in south London. I had gone to see a queer cabaret, and took a break outside partway through with a couple of friends. A man who was smoking in a group nearby took it upon himself to call out to us: "How are you doing tonight, lezzers?" It's true that a few people in our the group were lesbian-identified, but I had been trying to stand up for myself more often.

"I'm actually a man," I replied. "Making it difficult to be a lesbian."

"You're a man?" he scoffed. "Well, you probably don't have what I like in a man."

I just shrugged. I didn't think it mattered, since I had no plans on hitting on him.

•••

Later on, after I did start dating men, I was in Denver walking through a mall with a friend I hadn't seen in a while. This

175

friend was also trans. The fluorescent lights gave all of the beige tiles on the floor a surreal glow and made a cardboard cutout of Justin Bieber look like an angel. We clicked our heels past him, chatting away. It had been a while since I had been around any other trans people, and my shoulders felt a bit lower than they had been before. My friend was explaining to me that one of her gay male friends who lived there was single and that he kept complaining that there were no hot men around to date.

"Why don't you set me up with him?" I asked. "I'm here all weekend."

She looked at me with wide eyes, like she felt a bit wounded on my behalf, and said, "Oh honey, I don't think he dates men like you."

I tried not to look as hurt as I was.

• • •

When I got back home to Montreal, I downloaded Grindr, the gay men's cruising app. I had seen a friend use it and he was talking endlessly about all the dates he had gone on since he had joined. I thought it might provide me with a window into the world of gay male cruising without the immediate dismissal I had experienced from friends and at men-only gay clubs because of my appearance and voice. The first time I used the app, I was in my room in the St. Henri share house I lived in. I watched as the pictures and descriptions of men popped up inside the little orange squares on my phone. A lot of images were of bare-chested torsos, or barely-above-the-crotch shots. I tapped on one of the profiles closest in vicinity to me and almost jumped when I saw that he was currently only twenty-five meters away. He could have been as close as two floors above me. The possibilities of online cruising hit me like a wave. I uploaded a photo of myself and wrote "29. Montreal" as my description, then went to sleep. When I opened Grindr again in the morning, I saw that I had a message from a guy whose handle was "Buffalo." All it said was: "U R Cute. I am 5'10 250lbs 7 inches. Do U have more pics?"

I hadn't thought about the fact that I might be asked for some more revealing photos. I couldn't help but write a reply in my head: "5'3", 120lbs, dickless."

The next day I got another message: "29. Wow U look so young!"

I chuckled to myself. The guy in the photo looked really sweet and only had "NSA" (no strings attached) as his description. I decided I could handle replying to this one and typed: "Thanks."

After I pressed send, though, I got a bit anxious wondering if there was some sort of abbreviation for the word thanks that I didn't know about. Maybe I had already given away my status as a newbie to Grindr.

Then I got another response from him: "What are you up to tonight?"

This was the longest interaction that I had with a gay guy I hadn't met before. I decided to act casual and replied: "Not much."

"You're cute. We should meet up?" I felt myself blush. I looked at his photo again. He was cute. An earnest-looking young bear in a red and black plaid shirt with a septum piercing. Probably thirty-five-ish. Probably rode a fixed gear bike. I replied, "Sure. I could meet you for a drink downtown?"

After I sent the message, my skin started to prickle and my hands went a bit numb. I thought about my hairless face and high voice. He was going to notice those things right away.

Moreover, the particular alignment of my body parts might come up as unexpected to him if we did get along. I thought it might be good to give him a heads up. So I typed: "Just so you know, I am trans. Still a man, though, and gay."

I pressed send and left Grindr open on my phone for a while. After fifteen minutes when there was no response, I closed it and tried to forget about the conversation. After twenty-four hours and still no response, I started to understand that the clear rejection was based on my being trans. I then changed my profile to read: "29, Montreal, Trans man." I thought it was a good idea to get that out there before we got to chatting. I was not ashamed of being trans, and I was sure that some men wouldn't mind, or might even be trans themselves. That's when my Grindr comments started to look more like the comments to my YouTube videos, things like "Have U had UR sex change operations yet?"

A few days later, I was feeling defeated, but then I remembered that there were a lot of trans people like me who were interested in gay relationships and were probably on Grindr. I changed my profile description again, this time to read: "Trans 4 Trans. Queer 4 Queer." My new description solicited just as many ignorant questions about my body, gender, and legal sex as did my old description, but at least the other trans men would know that I was looking for them.

I did eventually date men, though I met them through friends in the queer community. Being trans is often designated as both my gender and my sexuality. Allowing me to choose what gender I identify as and fully respecting my choices would logically mean allowing me to also express my sexuality whether it be straight, gay, lesbian, bi, asexual, or queer, but it doesn't always happen that way. There are many people who are respectful and don't assume my sexuality or gender based on my presentation, and there were gays along the way who certainly allowed me to be a gay man in every sense. It was the ignorance that I encountered from many members of my own community that reminded me that I would not be accepted by every single gay person in the world. There are so many rules placed on physical bodies in the gay community, and being trans is certainly not the only barrier to acceptance. I prefer now to find the acceptance I need in the communities that are addressing discrimination.

After that show in London, I had an interview with some folks from a local LGBT paper in England. One of their questions was, "Do you play music to get the ladies?" I just laughed and didn't respond. Of course I dated female-identified people, but that had never been the reason why I had taken up the guitar. Back when I learned my first chords, I was hoping to become a Christian contemporary music star. But now I was so far from wanting to be a Christian singer that I preferred not to put any limitations on the future. I could have said I was a gay man to be contrary, but I knew it wasn't a representation of my identity either.

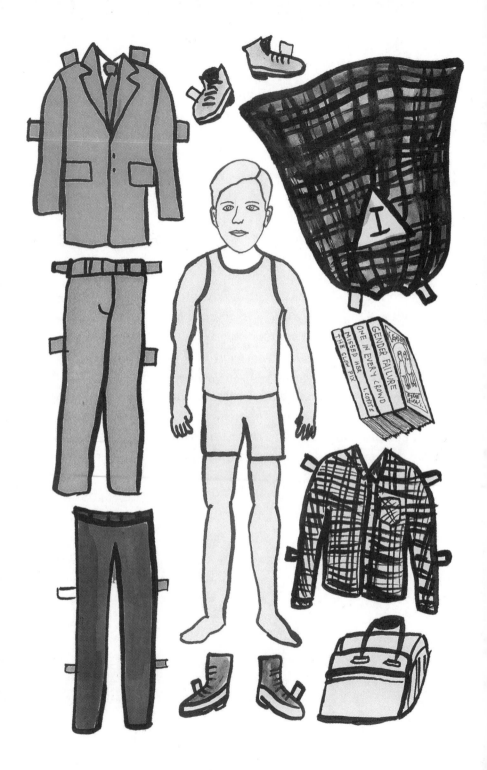

Many Moons

Six weeks post top surgery, I flew to California to teach memoir writing for a week in a summer arts program. My nipples were healed well into the safety zone, my scars were smiling pink, and I could lift my suitcase on my own, albeit carefully. I had agreed to the gig when the course coordinator had asked me the previous fall, mostly because one of the other instructors was a writing hero of mine whom I really wanted to work with: Lidia Yuknavitch, the author of the heart-busting memoir *The Chronology of Water.*

Because of availability and scheduling, I ended up teaching for the first week of the program, and Lidia was slotted for the second week. We were only going to have one night where our calendars crossed. She was to arrive late on the Sunday afternoon and I was flying out first thing on Monday morning. This was disappointing for a couple of reasons: the first one being that I really had been looking forward to teaching alongside a writer who could write so beautifully from inside the blood and guts of it all like Lidia could. And then there was the swimming thing.

Lidia's book was about healing from trauma and pain and loss by swimming through it and surfacing for air, partly cleansed and wholly reinvented. She writes about literally plunging into water as a means of reclaiming one's body from the people and things that took it from you.

I had not yet been swimming in this new body. Hadn't felt the water streaming over my flat and scarred chest. Who better to swim with for the first time than her? If anyone could understand the freedom, the release, the significance of that first submersion, it would be Lidia. I had originally dreamed of a midnight jump into the ocean, a fantasy I quickly edited on my first day in Monterey when I ran down to the Pacific Ocean and saw all the warning signs for undertows and deadly currents, and then stripped and let the waves crash into me waist-deep and icy cold, even for a Yukon kid. My fantasy hadn't included renting a neck-to-toe wetsuit, or drowning unceremoniously in the dark. It was all about the naked. The skin. The water on me, over me, around me. The outdoor pool on campus closed at four p.m., and Lidia didn't arrive until six. I was going to have to improvise something. I began to formulate my covert plan.

First I had to meet her, and see if she would be game.

We were both scheduled to attend a faculty dinner, in a hotel ballroom with circa 1987 carpeting and a view of the city and ocean, complete with a piano player and buffet dinner. I wore a shirt and tie and herringbone jacket, and she was in a lovely summer dress.

I introduced myself, feeling uncharacteristically wet-palmed and dry-mouthed. She shook my hand, and immediately confessed that she was kind of nervous about meeting me.

"Me too," I admitted. "Seriously. I am a pretty big fan of your work."

"No, really. I'm a fan of your work," she said solemnly.

"No, seriously," I repeated. "I even teach your work in my classes."

"I teach yours, too." She looked me directly in the eye, and then promptly spilled a large dollop of pasta sauce that somehow got into her long hair and onto the white tablecloth.

That is exactly when I knew she would be game.

Three complimentary glasses of wine later, we had sketched out the plan. Kimberly, fellow author and our course coordinator, was going to come along as well. I had explained to her that what two of her staff were about to do was illegal and possibly dangerous, and that for her to allow us to attempt said crime without supervision would be reckless and irresponsible.

I had printed up a map of the campus before leaving home, and for some reason had slipped a small but potent flashlight into my briefcase. I took this as a sign that the universe was smiling down on our plan.

It was just before midnight when we crept across the field next to the pool, Kimberly's flip flops slip-slapping at her heels, and the slim but sharp beam of the flashlight bouncing on the sand and grass in front of us. Betowelled and giggling, we had to leave the car parked outside the locked gate of the parking lot next to the pool. A bit of a heat score, and I knew this, but filed it away in the back of my mind under "Deal with this later."

Slowly the fence around the pool emerged from the black night outside my flashlight beam. It was twelve feet high, and apparently we were not the first to consider climbing it, because there was also a kind of a mesh tarp zap-strapped tight as a skin on the outside of the chain-link, to foil any possible toe and finger holds.

"I'm a big girl," Kimberly half whispered. "There are at least twelve reasons I can think of right now why I can't climb that thing."

Lidia nodded.

I let out a sigh, then took a deep breath. "Let's just walk the perimeter," I insisted. "Check all the gates."

They followed, but I could feel the wind in their sails sagging a little.

All the gates were locked, of course, and the locking mechanisms were attached to black pads that used identification cards for entry, all of which flashed red for no-go in the night.

All except for the gate at the very back, right next to the maintenance shed. It only had a locked door. The deadbolt stuck out a bit like a tongue before it entered the latch hole, like it was egging me on.

"Who has a credit card on them?" I whispered, and the clouds parted a little to let the full moon shine down on us, like another sign.

"I do," laughed Lidia. "But it's maxed right out. If it works, that will be all it's good for. Jimmying locks."

She passed it to me, and I slipped it between the posts and nudged the bolt of the lock with it, praying that if I dropped it, it would land on our side of the fence, as her name was embossed right on it. Heat score number two.

The bolt slid aside with a smooth snick, and the gate swung open. We all stood there for a minute, faces split with wide grins, and then slipped inside.

There is always a chance that when you really build up an event in your head beforehand, that reality will pale by comparison. This was not one of those times.

The steam danced and swirled under our hands as we pulled back a corner of the pool covering. The full-the-next-night moon hung like a high beam right above us as we stripped and shivered a little, and then all jumped in as one. The water was warmer than I imagined it would be, and my heart pounded joy under its thin layer of healing skin. We swam and laughed and swam, coming together for one triple, treading-water hug. Just three bodies, unencumbered and uncovered.

I floated on my back for a long while, and felt one thousand remembered swims flood back into my body. A twelve-year-old body. An eight-year-old body. My five-year-old, flat-chested frame, tiny cold-numbed fingers on a sun-weathered dock. The smell of coconut-scented lotion and hot dogs and red Kool Aid and bug dope. Scratchy towels off the clothesline. Campfire heat on my sunburned face. All those swims in my before body.

After about twenty minutes, my spidey senses started to hum. "I think we better get out soon. The campus cops are bound to drive by and see the car parked outside the gate. Where else could we be but right where we are?"

We climbed out and dressed, quiet now and close to reverent. For some reason I put my tie back around my neck and tightened the half-Windsor under my chin, completing my costume.

Sure enough, a cop car pulled up and stopped when we were twenty feet away from escaping into Kimberly's car, and I heard a large pop as the officer focused a blinding handheld spotlight on us. My hands squeezed my wet towel, which I held dripping behind my back.

"What are you doing here?" a deep voice demanded from inside the solar flare.

I cleared my throat. "I was just taking these ladies out for an evening stroll. After the faculty dinner. Just heading back to the dorm right now." Paused to swallow. "You have a good night, officer."

The spotlight popped off, and the face that belonged to the voice appeared as my pupils dilated. Brush cut. Biceps. Both of them. They stared silent at us for a minute, and then rolled on.

I waited until the cop car was a block away before I turned to look at my co-conspirators. They both had long, sopping wet hair, and they both still had their towels around their necks. Two long-haired, dripping wet heat scores.

We laughed all the way back to my dorm room, where we sipped bourbon from a flask, only the sand between our toes and the smell of chlorine on our skin remaining as evidence.

Drag Failure

If there is one thing I have failed at as hugely as the gender binary, it's drag. In the beginning, my motivation to try drag was for an elaborate prank I wanted to pull on the music industry. A friend of mine wanted to make a music video for one of my songs, and we were exploring funding options. A certain music video grant came up and I joked that I was probably eligible, but that to be safe we should send a picture of a female model instead of me. I had been told by some people in the same organization that my image wasn't "commercial" enough for that type of funding. I have always found it hard to present as commercial in an industry that has very few accepted models for women, let alone for trans folks. I couldn't help but wonder if it was my appearance that was a large part of the problem. This conversation with my friend then turned into joking. What if we sent a picture of me in drag as a woman to the organization funding this music video grant? That was a good one. I hadn't been in a dress for longer than I could remember. We laughed ourselves silly, drank more coffee, and then hatched a more elaborate plan. What if I recorded the same album twice and released it first as myself, but then as another persona that was me in drag? My friend could then film a documentary about it. And that is how Cocolene, my female-impersonating drag persona, was born.

The idea of the prank made me giddy and I got to work on a group of songs that could be recorded by both a trans indie folk singer and a female powerhouse pop singer. (That's how most of the material for my album *Love Is A Hunter* was conceived.) As I worked, I tried to envision how I would pull off being in drag. I had never even worn earrings, as I had always resisted the peer pressure to take a trip to the mall with friends to get my ears pierced. I decided that this would be my first step, but that I only wanted to do one ear at time in case I didn't like it. I decided on a fake diamond stud at a piercing parlour in downtown Montreal. But when I looked in the mirror after it was done, I thought I looked more like a gay man than a fancy lady. Still, I figured I could go back and get the other ear done after I got used to the first one.

Next, I wanted to try to learn how to walk in heels, so I borrowed a pair from a friend with the same shoe size, but unfortunately I was over-confident and chose the highest ones she owned. When I put them on, I found myself barely able to stand, and I had to clutch at the wall of my kitchen. After the click of my first brave step, I heard the scrabbling sound of claws from the other side of the loft. Suddenly my roommate's chihuahua came out of nowhere and attacked my feet. Apparently the small dog had experienced some trauma around heels, but as I tried to calm him down without falling over, I felt it wasn't a very good omen as far as my efforts at female impersonation were concerned.

I decided I needed more help. I told Kaleb, one of my best friends, about my plan to do drag. Kaleb lived in Toronto. He was the best drag queen I'd ever seen, pulling off fabulous stunts and wowing crowds as Miss Fluffy Soufflé. He was also trans, and I knew he would appreciate the nuances needed to impersonate the gender we were striving not to be read as in day-to-day life. Besides, who better than one of my best friends to help me be reborn as Cocolene? Kaleb and I decided that the best way for him to show me the ropes was for us to start our own fake band. We would do a photo shoot, perhaps write some songs together, and see where it went. He knew a great photographer that we could work with who had taken some photos of Fluffy. Luckily, Kaleb's partner Andrya happened to be the same dress and shoe size as I was, so I didn't have to buy myself a whole new wardrobe. It all fell into place just like it was meant to be.

During my next trip to Toronto, I hastily tried on a few of Andrya's heels and dresses, as well as a couple of Kaleb's wigs. We then all jumped in a cab to the Village for the photo shoot. I was gripped with excitement. The photographer was a kind gay man whose partner did amazing bear drag. He did slip and refer to me as "she" a couple of times while he did Kaleb's makeup, but I wasn't going to let that stop Cocolene's big moment. I changed into my dress while I waited, and then he went to work on my makeup. All of the powders and eyeliners and brushes were so new to me. Two minutes in, my face stopped smelling like it was my own. When he was done, he stood back and looked at me with a surprised look, saying, "Wow! You really look like a man with makeup on." I took this as a compliment and blushed. I wasn't sure if I should feel more masculine, more feminine, or both.

Then it was on to the shoot. Kaleb had a lot of great advice as we posed together, such as "Smile like you're biting into a hamburger!" I listened closely because he was the best, and at first I was cordial. I didn't mind photo shoots. I was into it, and I was trying really hard. But then I started to feel … something. It felt as though a fire alarm was going off three buildings over, or as if I'd left my oven on in Montreal. Something was definitely wrong. I looked around, wondering what it could be, before slowly focusing my eyes down at myself. It was the heels and the dress! It was Cocolene! It felt like someone was pinching my arm, the kind of pain that's easy to endure at first but eventually wears a person down.

My whole concept for the album was in jeopardy. In one last effort, I decided that if I could go out as Cocolene in public, then I could stand to spend a couple of years living as her, releasing an album as her, and touring as her across the country. I had promised a couple of my friends in Montreal that we would all dress up and go out to the drag bar in the gay village. So one night I put on a wig, a dress, and heels, and one of my friends who did makeup helped me put on some lipstick and blue eyeshadow. We took a bus downtown. At first I was holding it together, but before we got to the bar I started getting the same weird feeling that I'd had at the photo shoot. I almost picked a fight with a guy who looked at me funny on the street, shouting, "What are you looking at?"

I was wearing a huge blonde wig with over-the-top makeup. If it had been light enough for me to see myself in the reflection of a downtown window, I could have observed the answer to my own question. One of my friends called me Courtney Love because of it, and I took it the wrong way. By the time we made it to the drag bar, I was really angry at whoever it was who was making me feel so bad. A quiet moment in the ladies' washroom helped me think clearly. It was me who was the culprit. It was being Cocolene. I reflected on how I had been forced to wear dresses to church every Sunday until I was sixteen. I could see where some of the rage was coming from, and there was a limitless supply. There was only one thing to do. No more drag. And, definitely, no more Cocolene.

These days, Cocolene is gone. Sometimes I tell my friends that she went on a long trip. I'm glad I tried drag, even though it made me so uncomfortable. Not every trans person can be Fluffy Soufflé. I'm just not as fabulous.

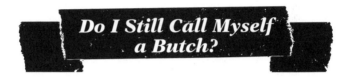

Do I Still Call Myself a Butch?

Yes. Of course I still do.

*T*oday at the market, I spotted a wicked handsome silver fox of an older butch. She caught me looking at her, twice, so while we were standing next to the yogurt section together, I took a deep breath and said: "I don't mean this in a weird way or anything, but I am in a butch choir, and we are a fairly dapper lot, and there are like, twenty of us, and even still, you are the handsomest thing I have seen all week." Then I panicked a little inside, I mean, what if she didn't like the word butch? What if she was straight? I mean, she was wearing her post office uniform, but even still, you never know, right? But she smiled at me, showed the wrinkles around her eyes, laughed low and then said: "Handsome? Well, thank you for that. You just made my day." She even had dimples. Fucking dimples kill me.

Who do you think you're fooling

C#m   E
We've been running all our lives
C#m   E
looking for something that feels right.
C#m   E
We've been running all our lives   E
C#m   E
looking for something that feels right.

                              C#m
But you say: who do
                                        E
Who do you think you're fooling?
                C#m
         Who do
                                    E
Who do you think you're fooling?

It's not up to you to decide.
It's not up to you to decide.
It's not up to you to decide.
It's not up to you to decide.

So don't say: who do
Who do you think you're fooling?
                Who do
Who do you think you're fooling?

How I Got to "They"

The first time I heard the pronoun "they" used for a single person, I was in Montreal, and I was being corrected on how I was referring to someone.

"Do you know any good guitar players around? I just moved here and I'm looking for people to play music with," I asked a guy I had just met.

"Do you know Jen?" he asked.

"Yeah, does she live here?" I inquired.

"Yeah, but actually Jen goes by the pronoun 'they,'" he responded.

I was stunned. Correcting pronouns was something I was used to being on the opposite end of, and I hadn't perceived the person as trans at all. I thought that a traditional female name or femme presentation automatically denoted that an individual was a woman. I had spent ten years trying to convince people to refer to me as "he," which was the same number of years as the person using "they" was younger than me.

"I don't know about that," I said dismissively.

"What?" the correcting party asked.

My stomach churned. I felt weak, like I wanted to yell and swing at the air. "I mean, I think it would be pretty hard to get people to actually call you that outside of the queer community," I said, and changed the subject.

But the interaction stayed with me and replayed itself over and over. The ten years of being out as a trans man went through my mind, along with all of the repetitive explaining and requesting of the "he" pronoun, and the distance that not being accepted as male put between me and most others. All of the places I stole away to whenever people who had known me for years slipped up or refused to change. The invisibility of not even being considered trans at all by some members of the trans community because I had not changed my body with hormones or surgery. I had been fighting to cross over to the other side of the gender binary, and this person was just going to sit out of it altogether? A disregard for the gender binary felt like my experience was being taken from me. Yet, I knew my response had put me on the side of those who refused or dismissed other people's identities. Treating people like they had to earn their gender was the very thing I had been fighting against. I couldn't shrug off the feeling. I couldn't understand it fully, but I wanted to try. I had asked that of so many people myself.

I found it hard at first to use "they" as a pronoun for others. I was embarrassed when I would skip from "he" or "she" to "they" in a sentence, watching my tongue struggle awkwardly to shape the right pronoun. It was especially difficult when I felt that the person's name didn't contradict their assigned gender, or if they hadn't changed their name at all. It made me feel like I was back at the beginning of learning a new language. Words volleyed from my brain to my mouth and back as I tried to get it right. Here I was again learning pronouns even though I was trans, and had been trans for a long time, and thought I knew so much about trans people. It was humbling, and it made me start to rethink everything else I thought I knew.

What would it mean not to be a man or a woman? Over the years I had learned not to think of people's assigned sexes as their genders, but I had expected others to place themselves at least conceptually on one side of the gender binary. I started to meet a lot more people who went by the "they" pronoun. Most people in the queer community around me didn't have any difficulty using it. In a space where non-binary pronouns had been largely accepted, I began to see the benefits of using them. It dragged me out of an identity that had been previously cemented because I thought being a man was the only way to move away from my assigned sex. In this community I did not have to be male not to be female.

I began requesting that people use "they" for me in these spaces. Being called "they" freed me up to think about which parts of my behaviour had been constructed in order to convince people that I was a man. I thought a lot about how sexist the rules of the gender binary really were. Without the pressure to make my body more masculine in order to earn a pronoun, I started to think a lot about bodies. My whole platform about being a man but not modifying my body was that it was identifying as a man that made me male, rather than the sex of my body. That was the difference between sex and gender. In gender neutrality, I decided to refuse the model of body characteristics denoting sex and gender altogether. I wanted to call anyone any pronoun or name they wanted regardless of how I read their body, gender presentation, or behaviour. If only the rejection of the gender binary was more widespread. That was the only thing that would have made my new identity more relaxing. I knew what my first reaction had been, and that I was up against that reaction from others.

At first I was fearful of going public with my new preferred pronoun. I still felt that making this request anywhere outside of the queer community was going to be like telling people that the robots had landed. I had spent so much time explaining my gender as a trans man to strangers on tour and to the media. Being trans was far more of a topic in interviews I did than the music I made. I wasn't sure if I was up to coming out all over again with a far less recognized pronoun. I saw the way that coming out as transgendered had affected what spaces I was invited to play in, and I worried that rocking the boat further would end my career for good. So I decided to continue going by "he" professionally. I did that for a few years. I continued to ask for people to call me "he" when they referred to me as "she." It was the same difficult fight it had always been. Then I played a festival that I had played ten years earlier and the pronoun usage was actually worse than it had been the first time. Had nothing changed? I realized then that I was always going to have to fight for my pronoun, and if I was going to have to do that anyway, I should be fighting for the one that made me the most comfortable, rather than a compromise that I thought would be more accepted.

I began to see other artists challenging the media to use this gender-neutral pronoun. The boycott, led by Elisha Lim, of a Toronto gay and lesbian newspaper after it refused to use their preferred pronoun, citing grammar considerations, in-spired me. I had been invited to be interviewed in the paper that month, but decided that instead I would also boycott them and write a Tumblr post about my disappointment in their decision. In this post, I also came out as preferring the "they" pronoun. The subsequent media reaction to my request surprised me. I released an album a month later and did a nationwide publicity campaign for it. A lot of the journalists I spoke to had read my Tumblr post and didn't need a lot of convincing. Many of the mainstream papers in Canada were far quicker to respond positively to the use of my pronoun than the Toronto gay and lesbian paper had been.

Still, since coming out as preferring "they," a lot of the opposition I expected to encounter has happened. There are many people who cite it as confusing or incorrect grammar. I never bother indulging this argument by pulling out historical examples of its use or its dictionary definitions. Language is a living thing, and I find the attempts to preserve it from the threat of gender-neutral pronouns to be a transphobic reaction. There are many other preferred pronouns that are new to the English language that should also be incorporated as they are requested. I don't think that anything like grammar should have priority over what makes people comfortable.

I am optimistic about the future of my gender retirement. Taking the responsibility off myself to earn my pronoun and rejecting the sexist requirements of the gender binary have proved to be more comforting than going by the "they" pronoun is stressful. There are a great number of people working to change how gender is perceived in order to make more room for all gender minorities, and I am proud to be one of them. Whenever I feel challenged, I access the memory of my first reaction to the pronoun I now go by, and I remember that a lot of things can change.

Yesterday in the women's change room at the gym where I have been going for decades, I was referred to as a "freak of nature." The woman who called me this mistakenly thought I had left the room, but really I had just gone into the bathroom. When I walked back around the corner she just stared straight ahead, as if her ignoring me would make it all disappear. Would not meet my eyes. Amazing what nastiness and bigotry can seethe behind a blonde bob and a pair of yoga pants.

The Facilities

I can hold my pee for hours. Nearly all day. It's a skill I developed out of necessity, after years of navigating public washrooms. I hold it for as long as I can, until I can get myself to the theatre or the green room or my hotel room, or home. Using a public washroom is a very last resort for me. I try to use the wheelchair-accessible, gender-neutral facilities whenever possible, always after a thorough search of the area to make sure no one in an actual wheelchair or with mobility issues is en route. I always hold my breath a little on the way out though, hoping there isn't an angry person leaning on crutches waiting there when I exit. This has never happened yet, but I still worry. Sometimes I rehearse a little speech as I pee quickly and wash my hands, just to be prepared. I would say something like, I apologize for inconveniencing you by using the washroom that is accessible to disabled people, but we live in a world that is not able to make room enough for trans people to pee in safety, and after many years of tribulation in women's washrooms, I have taken to using the only place provided for people of all genders.

But I have never had to say any of this. Yet. Once at an airport, I was stopped by a janitor on my way out who reprimanded me for using a bathroom that wasn't meant for me, and I calmly explained to him that I was a transgender person, and that this was the only place I felt safe in, and then I noted that there were no disabled people lined up outside the washroom door, or parents with small children waiting to use the change table.

He narrowed his eyes at me. Then he said, "Okay, but next time you should ..."

I waited for him to finish. Instead, he shook his head and motioned down the empty hallway with his mop handle that I should be off, that this conversation was now over.

I wondered later in the departure lounge exactly what it was he felt I should do next time? Hold it longer? Not have bodily functions at all? Use the men's room? The ladies'? Be someone else? Look different? Wear a dress? Not wear a tie? Cease and desist with air travel altogether? Do my part to dismantle the gender binary to make more room for people like myself?

I could write an entire book about bathroom incidents I have experienced. It would be a long and boring book where nearly every chapter ends the same, so I won't. But I could. Forty-four years of bathroom troubles. I try to remind myself of that every time a nice lady in her new pantsuit for travelling screams or stares at me, I try to remember that this is maybe her first encounter with someone who doesn't appear to be much of a lady in the ladies' room. That she has no way of knowing this is already the sixth time this week that this has happened to me, and that I have four decades of it already weighing heavy on my back. She doesn't know I have been verbally harassed in women's washrooms for years. She doesn't know I have been hauled out with my pants still undone by security guards and smashed over the head with a giant handbag once. She can't know that I have five cities and seven more airport bathrooms and eleven shows left to get through before I can safely pee in my own toilet. She can't know that my tampon gave up the ghost somewhere between the security line and the food court. I try to remember all that she cannot know about my day, and try to find compassion and patience and smile kind when I explain that I have just as much right to be there as she does, and then make a beeline, eyes down, shoulders relaxed in a non-confrontational slant, into the first stall on the left, closest to the door.

Every time I bring up or write about the hassles trans and genderqueer people receive in public washrooms or change rooms, the first thing out of many women's mouths is that they have a right to feel safe in a public washroom, and that, no offense, but if they saw someone who "looks like me" in there, well, they would feel afraid, too. I hear this from other queer women. Other feminists. This should sting less than it does, but I can't help it. What is always implied here is that I am other, somehow, that I don't also need to feel safe. That somehow their safety trumps mine.

If there is anything I really do understand, it is being afraid in a public washroom. I am afraid in them all the time, with a lifetime of good reason. I wish that I had some evidence that harassing people in public washrooms really did originate from being afraid. I wish I could believe them that it starts with their own fear. What I suspect is more true is that their behaviour begins with and is fed by a phobia. They are afraid of men in a women's washroom, because of what might happen. I am afraid of women in a women's washroom, because of what happens to me all the time.

I don't see cisgendered women who want to feel safe in

a public washroom as my adversaries, though; what I see is the potential for many built-in comrades in the fight for gender-neutral, single-stall locking washrooms in all public places. Because the space they seek and the safety I dream of can be accomplished with the very same hammer and nails. Because what I do know for sure is that every single trans person I have ever spoken to, every single tomboy or woman who wears coveralls for her job or woman with short hair or recovering from chemo, or effeminate boy, or man who likes wearing dresses, or man with long hair that I have ever met is hassled or confronted or challenged nearly every other time they use a public washroom, anywhere. Always. Often. Every day. All the time. Incessantly. Repeatedly. Without mercy or respite. Every thing from staring to pointing to screaming to physical violence.

This violence and harassment is justified by people claiming that they were afraid. But very rarely does it feel to me like the person harassing me is actually afraid. Startled, maybe, for a second or two. But when I explain that I was assigned female at birth, just like they were, they usually don't back down. Their fear doesn't disappear, or dissipate. This is right about the time their friend will shake their head at me as if to say, what do you expect? They will pat their friend on the back to comfort them. They both feel entitled to be in a public wash-room, entitled enough that they get to decide whether or not I am welcome there. This feels to me like I am being policed, and punished for what I look like. This doesn't smell like fear to me. It reeks of transphobia.

It starts very early. I know a little girl, the daughter of a friend, who is a self-identified tomboy. Cowboy boots and caterpillar yellow toy trucks. One time I asked her what her favourite colour was and she told me camouflage. She came home last October in tears from her half-day at preschool with soggy pants because the other kids were harassing her when she used the girls' room at school and the teacher had instructed her to stay out of the boys' room. She had drunk two glasses of juice at the Halloween party and couldn't hold her pee any longer. She and her peers were four years old, they knew she was a girl, yet already they felt empowered enough in their own bigotries to police her use of the so-called public washrooms. I find it extremely hard to believe that these children were motivated by fear of another little girl. She was four years old and had already learned the brutal lesson that there was no bathroom door with a sign on it that welcomed people who looked like her. She had already been taught that bathrooms were a problem, and that problem started with her, and was hers alone.

My friend asked me to talk to her, and I did. I wanted to tell her that her mom and I were going to talk to the school and that it would all stop, but I knew this wasn't true. I wanted to say that it would be better when she got older, but I couldn't. I asked her to tell me the story of what happened. Asked her how it made her feel. Mad and sad she told me. I told her she wasn't alone. She asked me if I had ever peed in my own pants. I told her yes, I had, but not for a long time. When you get bigger, your bladder grows bigger too, I told her. When you get old like me, you will be able to hold your pee for a lot longer, I promised her. Until you get home? she asked me. I said yes, until you can get home. She seemed to take some comfort in that.

So I get a little tired of having to swallow my lived experience to be force-fed someone else's what-ifs. I get tired of my safety coming second. I get tired of the realities of trans and gender non-conforming people's lives being overshadowed and ignored in favour of a boogey-man that might be lurking in the ladies room. I get really tired of being mistaken for a monster. I get tired of swallowing all these bathroom stories and smiling politely. But the last thing I can do is allow myself to get angry. Because if I get angry, then I am seen as even more of a threat. Then it's all my fault, isn't it?

Because then there is a man in the ladies' room, and for some reason, he's angry.

*J*ust for the record, glaring at me in disgust in the women's change room will not magically make me more feminine. Believe me, the stats are in on this. If dirty looks could make me conform, it would have happened long ago. Does it make you feel better? It sure doesn't add any charm to my gym experience, just so you know.

P.S. I probably should have told you that you had a period stain on the ass of your yoga pants, but you didn't seem all that approachable.

What Do You Think I Am?

I was sitting in the middle seat on the plane when I saw him coming down the aisle. His face was red and he had the look of a guy who had been sitting in the bar of the airport for quite a while. He stopped in front of me, and said, "Hey dude. I'm sitting in the window."

I stood to let him in and then sat back down, pulling my computer onto my lap. He looked at it, whistled to himself, and said, "Kids these days, eh? Fancy toys."

I looked at him. "I bet I'm older than you," I replied.

"No way. How old are you?" he asked.

"Thirty-one," I said, hoping I was right that he was younger.

"Whoa! I'm twenty-eight. Oh, man! You look so young."

And then I was certain he thought I was a man. I hadn't lowered my voice. I was wearing a pink button-down shirt. My legs were crossed in front of me. I wasn't trying to be read as male at all, but still I felt that I had somehow brought it upon myself. I decided to go along with it.

The flight continued and I gave him change so he could buy a beer. "Oh, man. They don't have any Molson Canadian.

Which one do you think I should get? Is this one good?"

"I think you should get a Grasshopper." I was more than familiar with Alberta beers.

"Cool. Do you want one?"

"Nah, I don't drink."

"I should be more like you and then I would look as young."

During the course of the flight, we continued to bond as he showed me pictures of big trucks on his phone, and had me hold his beer as he searched for a tin of chewing tobacco that he was certain he'd dropped on the floor. He never did find it. The whole time I was enjoying myself. It felt like I had travelled back in time and was hanging out with one of my uncles when he was in his late twenties. As the flight landed, my seatmate told me he'd been working on the oil rigs and was finally going home to Winnipeg after many months away. I told him I was going there to play a show. "Oh yeah? Where are you playing?" he asked.

I thought about it and decided to tell the truth. I was so tired of bothering to hide things.

"I'm playing at Gio's," I said. Gio's was the gay bar downtown.

"Oh." He paused. "I'm not allowed there anymore. I used to deliver pop there and you know ... I can't come to your show. You understand, right?"

"Yeah, I do," I said, grateful that he was aware enough of his own homophobia to keep himself away from the gay bar.

And that was the end of our friendship.

•••

The next time I got on a plane, I was late. My seat was at the very back. I could see the guy I had to sit beside because he was next to the only empty seat left on the plane. He was leaning all the way around his seat to talk to the flight attendant in the back. He didn't stand up to let me in, but moved his legs into the aisle instead. As I squeezed past he said, "Here you go, lady."

I looked at him after I sat down, and said, "Lady? Why don't I call *you* lady?"

He turned his head and ignored me, still fixated on the flight attendant. "So is the diamond on that engagement ring real? You're just doing this for fun?"

The meaning of this was clear: Your future husband is rich. So, this is just some sort of last display of freedom before you get married and spend all of your time with the kids, right? The pilot's preflight announcements came on. I shifted so that my head was completely turned away from him.

"Oh my God. The pilot is a woman! That's weird, right? I mean, unusual?" the man asked the flight attendant.

I couldn't stay quiet. "What is so weird about a woman flying a plane? You're acting like you just found out that a giraffe is flying the plane." I spat the words at the back of his head.

"But is it unusual?" he answered me, directing it to the flight attendant.

She replied with the calm grace of someone who had a lot of experience dealing with jerks who wrap themselves around their seats to talk to her. "Sir, maybe you got the idea from television that only men fly planes, but we have a lot of female pilots working for the airline." She started listing them by name, and I smiled and turned my head back to the window.

• • •

I've been touring for more than ten years. Travel takes me out of the queer community of Montreal and into a world where I never know how people are going to read my gender. It usually takes me a while during an interaction to determine what people think I am, and sometimes I never quite figure it out. I don't know how old people think I am, or if they think I am male or female.

It's particularly hard for me to predict what gender people assume I am. Usually it's about half and half where people place me in the gender binary. I have had people address me as "ma'am" at the same airport where earlier I had been sent to the men's line for a patdown. I usually just try to float through without making a big deal out of it. If airline employees apologize for calling me "sir" after looking at my boarding pass, I often say, "That's okay. I mean, look at me." Sometimes this causes them to apologize more because they are upset that I don't feel bad about it. Gendered washrooms can also be difficult, but I just try to get in and out quickly without looking at anyone. It took me years to realize that a lot of people are just trying to be polite when they call me "ma'am" or "lady." I still tip them well and try to be kind. After all, I'm the only one who gets hurt when I get angry over the little things. Being called "lady" is not an insult as far as I am concerned. Sexism is what I find hard about being read female in public. I'm not insulted on my own behalf because I am transgender and being read wrong. I am angry about how women are treated. This can often lead to tense situations where I refuse to laugh things off or let men take up more space when they sit next to me on a plane.

During the course of one hour in an airport, I've been treated like I'm fourteen, twenty, and thirty. On a plane, I've been asked if I'm doing my homework and been given a children's meal. I usually shrug off any age discrepancies and go along with them (you better believe I'm going to eat a children's meal if it's right in front of me). Many people encourage me and tell me never to give up my dream when they see my guitar. I usually just nod, smiling. Some fellow travellers have become alarmed that I am touring all by myself, which does make me feel cared for even if I am forced to answer that I am unsure of my parents' whereabouts. This usually causes more alarm. I'm not angry when people think I'm young. Being young is not a bad thing. What I don't like about it is the way that a lot of people treat young people. I have had flight attendants bark at me as I board a plane calmly, or condescend to me about having overweight luggage or carrying a guitar. Fewer and fewer people think that I am a teenager, but as I move into my twenty-second year of being treated like one, I can see how the only way that youth can respond to hostility is with hostility. There isn't a lot of room for anything else when people treat you like they don't have to respect you.

Throughout the interactions I've had over the past ten years, I've learned that the gender binary is more of a comedy skit than a fact. People read each other, assign identifiers, and then play out a script accordingly. A lot of the time these interactions are absurd, playing themselves out on the ground and thirty thousand feet in the air in the same ways. Sometimes I want to ask people, "What do you think I am?" as soon as I lock eyes with them, but mostly I just want to get to where I'm going.

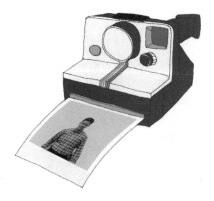

*J*ust gave the butch nod to someone I swore was a twenty-
something baby butch or genderqueer person working at the
grocery store up the street. Turned out to be a handsome young
teenage boy. He probably wonders why all the old dykes seem
to like him so much.

Their, There

Just recently I have started using the pronoun they. Asking people to refer to me by the pronoun they, to be more specific. This feels right enough, more right than he or she do, anyway. I wish we could figure out a way to talk to and about each other in this language that didn't involve constantly using a pronoun, but we haven't yet, so they it is. I'm not interested in having a conversation anymore about whether or not it is grammatically correct to use they as a singular pronoun, the least important reason for this being that there is published evidence proving it has been used as far back as the sixteenth century, and by the likes of Chaucer. More pressing than archaic grammar is the here and the now: language changes and evolves to reflect the culture of those using it, and some people wish to be referred to by the pronoun they. This is what makes them feel comfortable, and seen. That is really all the reason needed. The more I use they as an option, the easier it seems to get. I like not gendering my friends when I talk about them with others, it somehow lets their gender become a background detail, and allows other, more personal and relevant details about them shine through, shine around and over the sexism and misogyny of our world and skirt around preconceived ideas of who they might be and what they might be capable of.

The other day, I was talking to my dad about my friend Carrie, the carpenter. I referred to Carrie as they, which allowed me to tell my father what a good carpenter they were (which they definitely are) without him stopping me to ask what? Carrie is a lady carpenter? My friend Carrie is anything but a lady, but she is a fine carpenter, however, in order to keep the conversation being about Carrie the carpenter, instead of whether or not Carrie is a lady, I used the "they" pronoun for her. In my dreams, I imagine a world where we use "they" to refer to everyone, unless for some reason their gender is important or relevant to understanding the conversation, which it almost never is. That Carrie. They are such a good carpenter. I told Jamie that the sweater they knit for me fit perfectly. That Ivan. They always were such a dreamer.

I still use the pronoun she for my publicity materials, and for mainstream media stuff, for two reasons: the first is that I do a lot of work in public schools, and I want those young women and girls to see every kind of she there can be. I want them to see my biceps and my shorn hair and shirt and tie and for some of them to see me as a possibility. For the ones that need to see other possibilities to see me, and recognize a future for themselves. I want them to see me living outside of the boxes, because they might be asphyxiating in their own box and need to see there is air out here for them to breathe, that all they have to do is lift the lid a little.

The second reason is that for the most part I find the media to be lazy. Or maybe overworked, if I reach for the compassion ring. In any case, I find that the majority of reporters don't really want, or are not provided the space or time or word count, to really understand their subject. That every person or event they write about or review must be reduced to talking points, a headline, and a pull-out quote. All too often this means I am reduced to a woman who looks like a man. Or a gender-blender or some other nonsensical and diminutive term. I am no longer an award-winning author of ten books, or a musician, or a performer who has been touring the world for nearly twenty years, or a storyteller. I am reduced to a sideshow attraction. I once had a reporter ask me if I had had any surgeries. I told her yes. I had an ingrown toenail removed in grade five, and I had to have my wrist re-broken and set properly once when I fell out of a tree, but that I still had my appendix and my tonsils.

She told me she knew I was going to say something like that. She said, "Come on, you know what I mean."

I told her to come right out and ask me what she was asking me.

So she asked me if I still had my breasts, or if I was planning to have a breast augmentation, or if I wanted to have a penis constructed, or my penis removed.

It was only then that I realized she didn't know what sex or gender I had been assigned at birth, so she couldn't even be sure what I might want removed or added on to me, but still. She had to know. She just had to ask.

"Beg your pardon," I told her. "I thought you were interviewing me because my novel about a heterosexual mechanic just won a national literary award."

There was a moment of silence. We finished the interview, but gone was her conversational, easy, friendly demeanor. After that, she talked to me like I was the one being difficult. Like I was the one who had asked a rude question.

So here it is. My friends call me he, or they. The government and most of my family call me she. The media calls me she, because I don't trust them enough to request that they do anything else. My lovers call me sweetheart. Or baby. Somewhere in all of that I find myself. These are all, after all, only words.

I am in the dining hall of the university campus where I am teaching. I get up to go and scrape off my plate and put it in the bus pans. There is a kitchen staff guy there sorting the dirty dishes. "Thank you, sir," he says as I put my dirty plate in the bin. Then he does a double take at me up close, and says, "Oh, I'm sorry. Thank you, miss." I smile at him. "Actually," I say, "I prefer sir." He doesn't bat an eyelash. "So does my mom," he tells me, totally deadpan. I am kind of in love with him now.

Touring Success and Touring Failure

I had just stepped off the stage at an Edmonton concert after an encore. The days of playing to empty rooms felt over. I was almost ready to admit to myself that I had gotten to a comfortable place with my job. I was heading to get my merchandise from the front of the room when a man grabbed me by the arm. He was a lot taller than me, and I jumped back out of reflex. He cocked his head, leaned down, and said, "You're gonna think this is hilarious!" I doubted it, but he still had me by the arm. "When I first saw you, I thought you were a dude, but when you started singing, I knew you were a chick!"

I made my best effort to keep my face blank lest any displeasure on my part be mistaken for aggression. I was too tired for anger and felt like the interaction had run its course. I just wanted to get my records and go to sleep. I pried his grip from my arm and started to walk away. As I left I turned my head and shouted: "Nice to meet you. You were mistaken both times. I'm transgendered." He stood motionless and then abruptly turned and walked toward the bar without a response.

Since I publicly changed my pronoun to "he" in 2001, this is how most of my concerts have ended. There are almost always a few interactions that temper the success with a feeling of failure, a feeling that I have failed to be seen.

The next day, I woke up to my cell phone alarm in the dim light of the hotel room's blackout curtains that wouldn't quite close. The familiar sound of my flip phone chiming didn't give me any clues as to where I was. I picked it up, and the screen said it was two p.m. I rolled onto my back and looked up at the ceiling, and then it came to me. I was in Prince George. I'd taken an overnight Greyhound from Edmonton. Upon my arrival at six that morning, I'd checked into this hotel in hopes of adding some deep sleep to the shallow naps I'd had intermittently all night on the bus. Like all modest hotel rooms I'd been in, this one had a tiny coffee maker, and I drank the hot liquid wondering who would be around to even go to my show that night. It was a Sunday evening on the Canadian Thanksgiving weekend.

Once I was dressed, I walked out into the sun hoping to find a place to eat. The smell of the pulp mills hit my nose just after the light. Right outside of the hotel there was a newspaper box and my own image caught my eye. It was tucked in the corner with the headline "TRANSGENDER PERFORMER COMES TO TOWN." I pried four quarters out of my pocket and opened the front of the box as the last one rattled down inside. I remembered doing the interview, but I thought it had been for the entertainment section, not the cover. I leaned on the box and read through the piece. The pronouns all seemed okay, but they had managed to talk about my gender for half of the article. There was nothing inherently transphobic about it, so I felt indifferent to its content. At least I was getting written about.

I tucked the paper under my arm and started to walk down

3rd Avenue. To my left were train tracks, and to my right everything was closed, including the bookstore I was supposed to play at later. I started to feel very alone. Looking at my face on the front of the paper again, I wondered if I'd used up one of my lives by asking my publicist to try to get me into the small-town papers on this tour. Was I in danger? I told myself to take a deep breath and stop worrying. I began ambling along a little slower in the same direction. It's not like everyone in the town would recognize me or anything. It was then that I saw the blue and red OPEN sign a little up ahead of me. It was hard to see it until I was right next to it in the bright autumn sun. It was the downtown bowling alley, but they were advertising food and I was hungry enough to give it a try.

Inside it felt dimmer in the fluorescent lights and it took my eyes a moment to adjust. All of the lanes were empty except for one. Two older couples in matching uniforms were bowling together, and far too absorbed in their game to notice me. I walked over to a line of orange vinyl spinning stools that sat in front of the wood laminate counter. There was a whiteboard with a scrawled menu that listed the daily specials. I stood as I read them and then slowly sat down, putting the paper on the floor near my feet.

An older guy in a bowling shirt with the name "Mick" embroidered on it walked up behind the counter from a back room. "Hey," he said. "Are you here to bowl?"

"Nah." I replied. "I just want to eat something."

"Okay. Do you know what you want?"

"Coffee and a grilled cheese sandwich, please." I said. He nodded and walked away.

I fiddled with a napkin from the dispenser in front of me, debating whether I should start writing my set list so early in the day. Mick came back with a cup of coffee in one hand and a bowl of creamers and sugar packets in the other. He had a different look on his face, a determined look that seemed bit more familiar to me. "So," he said, as he set the coffee down. "Are you the one in the paper?"

My blood pressure spiked. The words "Transgendered Performer Comes to Town" ran through my head. "Umm, yes," I said. I couldn't think of any other way to respond.

"Oh," he grunted. "Where are you from?"

"I grew up in Calgary," I mumbled, wondering if I should listen to the gnawing fear that was starting to rise in my stomach. I opened some sugar packets, trying not to spill them with my shaky hands, and dumped them into the coffee cup.

"Oh. I went to the Stampede there one year back in the eighties," he replied, his voice warmer in tone now.

"Yep. Every year in Calgary like clockwork," I said, stirring in some cream.

He deposited my food in front of me ten minutes later, including ketchup with my grilled cheese so I didn't have to ask for it, and tucked a handwritten bill under the napkin holder. I ate slowly, wondering how many people were going to recognize me in Prince George that day. I decided to go right back to the hotel after my meal and stay there until my show. I left ten dollars on top of the bill and walked out into the sunlight, heading back to my hotel, walking a little faster now.

That night there were many people at my show. Of all ages. I played the set list I had written on the hotel room's notepaper earlier that day as I watched TV. The crowd was subdued, but they seemed to be enjoying themselves. There was uniform applause between all the songs. The lack of alcohol in the venue kept everyone in their seats and quiet while I was playing. At the end of the show, while I was selling albums to fans, I saw a young person with his hands in his pockets, milling behind everyone nervously, and looking at me every so often. When everyone else had left, he walked up to me. "Hi," he said. "My name's Shawn. My parents saw you in the paper and brought me to your show." He gestured to two seated figures watching him from a few meters away. "I'm transgender too. F to M. I'm fourteen. I'm starting hormones next month," he finished, a little bit red in the face.

"Cool! Thanks for coming to the show," I said. "I'm thirty. I came out as trans about ten years ago. I decided that I wouldn't take hormones at first because of my voice and then later on because I feel okay with my body how it is."

"Well, it's all about what makes you feel comfortable, right?" he responded.

"Yep," I said.

We grinned at each other, and then went silent like we were both listening to something no one else could hear. His parents stood up looking like it was time to leave. He turned to go, and I said, "Hey, Shawn."

"Yeah?" he asked.

"Next time I play in Prince George, will you be my bodyguard?"

"For sure," he replied, looking a little bit taller, and then he turned and left with a parent on each arm.

Between the Boat and the Dock

I remember doing a show years ago in Seattle. Like, maybe the year 2000, somewhere around there. I still smoked cigarettes back then, and I was standing around in the drizzle on the sidewalk after the performance was over, having a smoke and talking to some friends. A woman approached me, thanked me for the show, and then leaned in to tell me how much she appreciated hearing herself represented as a proud butch woman in my words.

"It's getting rare these days, you know, stuff about being a butch." She shifted her eyes right and then left, and then lowered her voice so no one but her and I could hear it. "You know, as in not a trans man, but a butch woman."

I smiled and told her thanks, even though I often used the word butch to refer to myself, but didn't really use the word woman so much. And in my heart I identified with my trans male brothers just as much as I ever did with my butch sisters, and always endeavoured to never draw lines in the sand between us as she just had.

I had already spent years feeling like I was perched with one foot on a trans-shaped rowboat and the other foot resting on a butch dock, balancing myself and my language and words and work in the space between them.

I also knew that as an artist, my job was to create and present the work, and then stand aside and let everyone decide for themselves how to interpret my writing, and how much of it resonated with them, or didn't. I knew even then that the world is tragically devoid of enough words and work and images that represent butch reality in anything other than the butt of a your-mother-wears-army-boots joke. Butches are so often the punch line, and so rarely the subject, and almost never the hero. Who was I to challenge her interpretation and experience of my stories? She had seen herself in them, and took comfort and strength in that, and that to me was the point. Perhaps she had witnessed something other than what I had intended, but that didn't matter enough for me to take those rare and good feelings away from her. So I shook her hand firmly, looked her right in the eyes and thanked her, and I meant it.

Not sixty seconds after she had jumped into her Subaru wagon and driven off, a young man stepped up to speak to me. He thanked me for my words that night, and told me how important my work had been for him as he navigated his transition and found his place in his new body and identity.

"Thank you so much for representing trans guys without forgetting about feminism. I'm like you. I am a man now but I don't want to forget. I don't want to just transition and become another misogynist dude so I can pass."

Again, I thanked him and shook his hand. What purpose would be served by telling him I wasn't a man? That I wasn't just like him, that I didn't plan to transition, that I don't like or use the word "pass," that I reject the hierarchy that the word pass helps to create, that I resist the binary system and celebrate the lives and bodies of other gender failures like myself?

I knew if I were to find the time for the two of us to sit down and really talk, I might discover that our worldviews weren't really that different after all, it was just this limited language and the scarcity of shared meanings of words that made it seem like he had misinterpreted me.

So I chose to focus on what we shared, not what made us different, and told him how much I appreciated him coming out to my show. Then he asked me for a hug, so I gave him one, and I meant it.

For years I grappled with this balancing act, "she" stuffed into one front pocket of my jeans, and "he" rolling around in the other. Second-wave feminists raised one eyebrow at my masculine name, but never high enough that it kept them from hiring me for their well-paid women's day gig at the university, and I continued to write about my trans experience, but as long as I was still okay with being referred to by female pronouns, it never cost me much.

When I first met Rae Spoon, they were a young, queer-identified country singer. They went by the "she" pronoun and wore satin cowboy shirts and crooned about trailers and dirt roads and hoedowns and broken hearts. Rae was talented and funny and had an unmistakable, completely unique and beautiful singing voice. Their star immediately began to rise, and Rae's name started to make regular appearances on posters for major folk festivals all across the country. I loved Rae's music, and listened to their first demo CD on repeat in my little apartment for months.

I remember when Rae changed their pronoun to "he," and came out as trans. We had started doing shows together here and there, and had become friends. In 2007 we booked a tour together and collaborated on our first full-length project. By this time Rae was experimenting with indie rock and dabbling in electronica. Rae and I toured the *You Are Here* project quite a bit, singing and telling stories at some pretty big festivals and to sold-out theatres, and I watched as Rae struggled with good-old-boy union stage techs and straight sound guys as they repeatedly referred to Rae as she during load-ins and soundchecks and on stages, even when told multiple times what Rae's chosen pronoun was. Rae was always gracious and professional, and took it in stride, but I could see their face twitch almost imperceptibly every time it happened, and I knew it wore Rae down, and weighed heavy on their slender shoulders. I felt fiercely, sometimes irrationally protective of Rae, which was often maddening, because there was really no way I could effectively shield them from these multitudes of daily indignities. I worried that they might slowly bleed to death from one thousand tiny wounds.

We never expected much better from the mainstream straight art and music scene, and so neither of us were all that disappointed. They called Rae she and both of us ladies, and we swallowed it and did our jobs, and were grateful for the work.

What was hard was watching how the queer communities and the women's music scene handled Rae's trans self. What was hard was watching trans guys who I would have thought should know better misgender Rae during introductions. Watching Rae swallow their rage and slip their guitar strap over those shoulders and get up there and sing with that beautiful voice like their heart hadn't just been broken by someone who should have taken better care of his family.

I watched as fewer and fewer lesbians showed up for Rae's

shows, but still came out to mine. I watched for a couple of years as transphobia cost Rae in record sales and empty seats. The fact that Rae continued to tour the world, often by bus and mostly solo, and produce increasingly more nuanced and more widely received albums is a testament to not just their talent, but to their bravery and fortitude.

And me? I escaped being called the wrong pronoun by never choosing one, by telling myself over and over again that it didn't matter what anyone called me when they welcomed me to the stage.

Creating the *Gender Failure* show and writing this book together with Rae has been like a second chance for me. My second chance to stand shoulder to shoulder, right beside my beloved younger sibling, and offer my apologies that I was standing behind them the first time around.

Stories I Tell Myself and Others (Gender as Narrative)

More and more, I have thought of my gender as a story I tell myself. When I was assigned female, I told myself that I was a girl because it was the only information that I was given. There was no other option, so it was the only way. I struggled with the expectations that were placed on me, but the character I played was female, even if I was very bad at acting.

As a woman, I was attracted to other women. I would be in romantic couples where both partners were assigned female. I subscribed to the story that I was a woman who dated women, and that I was a lesbian. The people I dated believed that we were both women and that the relationship between us was a lesbian one. This was during a period where gays and lesbians were just entering the spotlight in mainstream media. There were newly accessible possibilities that could be incorporated into the stories we told ourselves.

When I came out as transgender, I started to tell myself that I was a man. I had the same body and the same history, but this changed everything. I told myself that I had always been male.

It made my difficulty at performing a female role make sense to me, but it also cancelled out the fact that I believed that I was a girl all along. I would say that I had never been a girl.

There was always a vetting period when I wasn't sure if the person I was romantically involved with really believed the story I told about my gender. For a transgender person, the difference is that we often have to sell our stories to other people, instead of assuming that our bodies, presentation, and gender assignment will do that work for us. I had always dated women, so I assumed I would continue that pattern. When I dated, I had to find partners who believed that I was a man and that they were women. It was a story we agreed upon. I was a man dating a woman. We were heterosexual. There were plenty of available narratives about heterosexual relationships to explore, but very few where the man was transgender. It was often hard to be accepted as male because of being trans-gender, so the story of my gender and relationships was often compromised by people who wouldn't respect my request to be accepted as male.

Then I started to date men. I had never been attracted to them when I was assigned female, but new attractions turned into reality, and I had to change the story again. I started to date people who believed that I was a man and that they were men. We were homosexual men together, and that was the story that we told ourselves. There were a lot of narratives about homosexual men that we could access to build the story of our relationships. I found it hard to be accepted as a man in the gay male community because I was, and sometimes my partners were, transgender. We were not welcome in male-only spaces, or accepted as a gay couple by other gay male cou-ples. In this way, the story of my gender and relationships were again invalidated a lot of the time.

I became tired of having to work for acceptance of my gender and relationships, especially from those who should know better. I started to think a lot about the barriers that had been imposed on me, and the things that had caused people to invalidate who I believed myself to be. What was it about me that made people read me as female? The way that people read me was often not what I was. Why did people often think that you can read anything about a person by their body? What makes people think that they can determine anyone's gender without asking them, or continue to misgender a person after a request not to?

All of my questions about being male and female led me to sexism. The general expectation for anyone to perform a gender role in the binary was based on polarized stereotypes for bodies, behaviour, and presentation. When looking at the reality of sex, there are variances from the stereotypes in almost every person assigned female or male. The ideal social expectations of gender are not represented in the general population, but they are enforced nevertheless. It was then that I gave up on changing my own body, presentation, or behaviour to match either side of the gender binary. I took the responsibility of earning acceptance off myself and stopped trying to convince people that I was male or female. I started to identify as gender-neutral and request that people use the "they" pronoun for me.

When I decided to retire from the gender binary, the narrative that I had about being a man stuck in a woman's body didn't make sense anymore, unless I was a gender-neutral person who'd been stuck in a man's body stuck in a woman's body all along. I started to consider that I was not essentially a gender, and that bodies should not be gendered based on the rigid binary system. I decided that my gender and sexuality had been a fluid narrative that I had constructed based on the options that I was given. I had not been a man or a woman for any reason other than that I had believed that I was one. Now that I had the option of opting out of the binary, the story could expand and evolve to include that identification as part of my history.

In practice, it is actually far more difficult to gain acceptance as a gender-neutral person. It's not a widely known identity, and gender is usually the most common identifier. With lovers, I still need an agreement on a story. I tend to request that we agree on a relationship that is not gendered at all. In public, I get a varied mix of perceptions. I never know if people think I'm a heterosexual man, a heterosexual woman, a lesbian, or a gay man. In practice, I have been all of these things at one time or another in my life. I don't find any one of them to be bad. Maybe my gender retirement is more of a "greatest hits"-style experience.

After all that has changed for me, I'm more inclined to leave the narrative open for myself than I have in the past. Now that I define my gender and sexuality as stories I tell and agree upon, I want to leave room for future possibilities that I have not been presented with yet. I am a gender failure. I failed at the gender binary, unable to find a place in being either a man or a woman with which I felt comfortable. But ultimately I believe that it's the binary that fails to leave room for most people to write their own gender stories.

danger danger danger

Dm
Danger, danger, danger. I'll be your sailor.
A
Write it on your body like we're out at sea.
Dm
Danger, danger, danger. I'll be your guide.
A/
Imaginary line between your chest and mine.

Dm   C
Glitter in my eyes. It's a dangerous love
                              A   G
We can hold each other up. We're surviving.

Danger, danger, danger. I'll be your failure.
You can make mistakes and I won't turn away.
Danger, danger, danger. I'll be your gay bar.
Yell it in your ear. Like we've never met.

Glitter in my eyes. It's a dangerous love.
We can hold each other up. We're surviving.

Danger

A guy strides right up to me and pokes me in the middle of my chest. "Are you a female?" He squints at me. "Kind of," I tell him. "What kind of an answer is that?" he asks me. "What kind of a question is that?" I ask him back, and then add, "And what kind of a man goes around poking strangers in the chest, anyway?" He nods his head, like he agrees with me on that point. Then he gets into a black and navy blue late seventies El Camino and drives away. I have a choice: to feel pissed off that he touched me like that, talked to me like that, or vaguely triumphant that he seemed to reconsider his behaviour, at least, if not apologize. I pick triumph. It was almost sunny that January morning, and way too early in the day to turn my day the wrong way.

I am a witness to a hit-and-run accident. It is dark and raining. A sports car hits a pedestrian and then screeches away. I call an ambulance, wait with the older woman while it comes. A policeman takes my name and phone number and address and writes them in his book. He narrows his eyes at me under the knife shape of light coming from the streetlight above us.

He appears to be considering something. "Do you, uh, have a gender?" he asks me. "Yes, I do," I tell him. A long couple of seconds of silence hang in the dark between us. "No need to be smart about anything. Are we going to have a problem here?" His words are clipped, severe, like his brushcut. "Hey," I say, "I'm the witness here. I stuck around. I called you guys. I thought I was the good guy." "Well, we can change that in a second if you don't co-operate," he informs me. "I am female," I tell him. "You're sure about that now?" he asks me. I don't say anything. "That's better," he says.

I am out to dinner with my sweetheart. She is wearing a little black dress and a rhinestone bracelet, and I am in a shirt and tie and dress pants. The waiter keeps mercilessly referring to both of us as ladies. Can I get you ladies some more coffee? Are you ladies going to have dessert? Can I bring you ladies the bill? I am obviously anything but a lady. I realize that the English language is sadly devoid of names for people like me. I try to cut the world some slack for this every day. All day. And the day after that, too. But the truth is that every time I am misgendered, a tiny little sliver of me disappears. A tiny little sliver of me is reminded that I do not fit, I am not this, I am not that, I am not seen, I can't be recognized, I have no name. I remember that the truth of me is invisible, and a tiny little sliver of me disappears. Just a sliver, razored from the surface of my very thick skin most days, but other times right from my soul, sometimes felt so deep and other days simply shrugged off, but still. All those slivers add up to something much harder to pretend around.

Any gendered public washroom, men's or women's, anywhere, anytime at all, every day of my life. Possible danger. I tell myself sometimes that if I did fit in a box, if there was always a bathroom for me, I would get bored, I would get soft,

I would lose my spidey senses, my cat-like reflexes, that the eyes in the back of my head would close forever and I would miss them. I tell myself this some days, but mostly I don't believe me.

Sometimes it exhausts me, all the head shaking and stumbling around to navigate and negotiate the two-ring circus that is this gender binary, walking pronoun tightropes and balancing between my safety and someone else's comfort. You are free to call me trans and I am proud to lift this name up and hold it, right there in the sun, and you would not be wrong, but this still feels like I am borrowing a word from someone else, that it is not all the way mine, really, and my friend who lent it to me might need it back, or they might need it more than me, and really, these are just words, and words are always imperfect, words are just sounds we make with our mouths that point our minds to think of things that cannot be fully described in words anyway. I am a writer, so I know where words fail us. A name is not a person, it is just what we have agreed to call them.

The thing about rarely been seen, the thing about always being called words that bounce off me or fall flat at my feet, is what a heart balm it is when she looks right at me like she does. How she heals me with that sideways flicker-in-her-eyes look. That you-just-wait-until-I get-you-home look. How her hands on me helped me own all of this body again. Her hands on me how she takes me takes what she wants and then gives it back to me when she is finished, gives it back to me better somehow. And I mean all of me. More whole. All the sweeter because it took so long for me to find myself, to truly live inside all of me.

Gender Retirement

To me, gender retirement is the refusal to identify myself within the gender binary. It's been a couple of years since I announced that I was changing my pronoun to "they" and renouncing my status as a man. It's not exactly how I pictured it turning out. I thought I might end up in some sort of Florida of gender with other retirees. Maybe I could spend my time sitting on a La-Z-Boy with a bubble pipe and a smoking jacket, watching the weather channel. I don't yet own a reclining chair like I had pictured, but I do spend a good portion of the day napping when I get the chance. I try to gather my strength for the periods of time when I meet people out in the world where my pronoun is rarely respected. I have thought of wearing a large button that says, "Hi. Please call me 'they,'" but I'm sure that would only result in being called 'Mrs. They' most of the time. My retirement from the gender binary seems to have left the rest of the world largely unaffected. Like a large, impersonal company that one's retired from, it seems to have moved on without providing me some sort of pension or even a certificate for the time invested. It feels more like being a sought-after secret agent. I can be minding my own business and then out of nowhere I am solicited to start participating again. The gender binary needs me! It's true that I can't escape it as long as I keep leaving my house, so perhaps resisting it is more like a full-time job, and a second career.

I don't mind being referred to as "he" as much as I do "she." Maybe because it's the most recent pronoun to the one I prefer. It's like a name I chose for myself and then ended up changing. After retiring, I stopped identifying as trans-masculine or anywhere on that spectrum. I loosened up my dress code, which was previously more about blazers, button-down shirts, and ties. I like to throw in a bright blouse here and there, and I tend to paint my nails if I feel like I am going to be particularly expected to behave like a man. It creates a dissonance with expectations that I enjoy. Gender-neutral fashion does not start and end with the masculine for me. I like to borrow from all sides of the spectrum, just as I shop in all parts of a department store for clothing. I shop in the men's and women's sections, cobbling together a look that could confound the most attuned gender-assignment identifier from a few feet away.

Being default gendered as a woman over half the time hasn't diminished in my retired state, although I am finding it easier to brush off. The thing that I can't brush off is that the most violent attack I ever experienced while on tour was because the attacker, a man who was a friend of the owner of the venue where I played that night, thought I was a woman and was being aggressive sexually. I managed to escape physical harm by calling 911 on my cell phone, but violence against women is not something that I am exempt from because I don't identify as a woman. Feminism, for the sake of the safety of all gender minorities, is always close to my mind and experience. Not being involved in the binary altogether makes the assignment as a woman feel more arbitrary than wrong. Most of my public interactions involve the immediate assignment as a woman, or the slow reveal of people discovering that they would rather assign me to the category of female. The slow reveal feels like a bit of a time-waster, and I have been known to skip over it if I need to match my assignment to the sex on my ID which reads "F." I sometimes tell people that the F stands for "Fuck Gender," but I am quick to let people assign me incorrectly if I need to get on a plane or cash a cheque. In these situations, my Gender Assignment By Convenience rule overrides my internal need to let people know about my retired state.

There is also the space of the in-between, which is the space that trans people live in no matter how they identify. A radio interviewer once asked me, "Do you feel more like a man some days and more like a woman on others?"

"No, I'm not really either," I said.

"Not one more than the other?"

Questions like this are used to insinuate that there is no way to live outside of the binary, only in-between its opposite poles. The whole point of changing my pronoun to the gender-neutral "they" was to state that I feel like neither. Yet almost every day, I am expected to declare myself as either a man or woman or, at the very least, somewhere in the spectrum in between. To me, gender retirement is very much about refusing to be put on that spectrum.

So far, I would highly recommend retiring from gender to anyone who is feeling like the spectrum or the binary doesn't fit. Many people look at me strangely when I tell them, but the decreased pressure of having to perform a gender makes up for all of the misunderstandings. I'm optimistic that living outside the binary will gain more recognition in the future, and so I mostly just bide my time when things get difficult. I don't think that gender retirement need only be available to people who identify as trans. Ideally, some sort of opt-out plan would be implemented for people who want to accept only part of their roles in the binary, but not buy into everything expected of them. There is no retirement home for gender, but I like to think that the less I expect others to conform to the expectations of the binary and the more I refuse to participate in it, the closer my dream of true gender retirement is to reality.

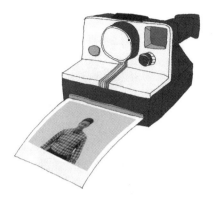

*T*oday *an old woman stopped me while I was walking the dog to tell me I looked a lot like her departed husband when she first met him in the fifties.* "He had good hair like you. He was a snappy dresser. Liked to take me dancing," *she said. Was he a good husband? I asked her.* "Good enough that I'm smiling at you fifty years later," *she told me.*

Ivan E. Coyote is a writer, performer, and author of seven books published by Arsenal Pulp Press: the story collections *Close to Spider Man, One Man's Trash, Loose End, The Slow Fix,* and *Missed Her*; the young-adult collection *One in Every Crowd*; and the ReLit Award-winning novel *Bow Grip*. Ivan is also the co-editor (with Zena Sharman) of the acclaimed anthology *Persistence: All Ways Butch and Femme* and, as part of the collective Taste This, co-author of *Boys like Her*. Ivan was a long-time columnist for the LGBT newspaper *Xtra!* Originally from the Yukon, Ivan is a resident of Vancouver.

Rae Spoon is a transgender musician and author originally from Calgary, Canada. They have been nominated for a Polaris Prize, toured internationally, and released seven solo albums, the most recent being *My Prairie Home* (2013). Rae is the author of the Lambda Literary Award finalist *First Spring Grass Fire*, and their essay "Femme Cowboy" was featured in the anthology *Persistence: All Ways Butch and Femme*. Rae is the subject of a National Film Board documentary-musical titled *My Prairie Home* (2013), which screened at film festivals internationally, including the Sundance 2014 Film Festival. They have also composed scores for films that have screened at Toronto International Film Festival, Sundance Film Festival, and Vancouver International Film Festival. Rae lives in Montreal with their partner, Kendra Marks.